I Love Me.
Who Do You Love?

A collection of stories, lies, loves, lists, letters, comics and other nonsense by

**DOUG
POWHIDA**

Copyright © 2017 by Doug Powhida

All rights reserved.

ISBN-13: 978-1542469203
ISBN-10: 1542469201

Dedication

For Sally, Greg and Annie – these words may not always be about you, but they are for you and because of you.

(Except for the endless sarcasm, the swear words, any mention of sex and the predictable disregard for decency. Other than that... 100% you.)

Acknowledgments

First and foremost, I am thankful to my wife, Miss Sally. There are few people in the world that would tolerate the person that has lived and written the following stories and articles. She was there for me before, during and, hopefully, after. Thanks for everything.

I'd also like to thank Lia Eastep who told me to start writing in the first place. When it was time to collect these stories, she was there with her editorial eye.

Both Michelle Ciappa and Jeffrey Stemen helped with the cover. I'd like to thank them both for making my head fit on the book without using a crowbar.

Thanks to all the readers of HolyJuan.com and Fake Dispatch. I do this for you. Well, I do it for me, but you liking it is what keeps me doing it for you, doing it for me.

And to Mom who always knew I'd be famous and to Dad who was the internet before there was there was the internet.

Backers

This book would not have been possible without the help of the following people that blindly pledged real money to help fund the publishing of these words. Thank you very much to all of you.

These backers are listed in no particular order except that Keegan is last:

Jeffrey Stemen
John "Two-Sack" Acton
Mary Lynn
Alan Burnstine
Mike Denison
John Baute
Neil
Steven DeGraeve
Matt Umland
Russ
Javier P.
Byron Gaudet
Dannielle Mosey
Mike
Stephanie Deal
Daniel Mosey
Karen Kress
Lauren Sheridan
Jerome Wetzel
Hugh & Molly
Molly & Hugh
Wooz
Beth Ann Kawalec
Chris Acton
Dave Briley
Ms. Mega Red Schofield
Metin Akin

Joseph
Dominic Messerly
Brad Allgire
Dana (Sofranko) Togliatti
Princess Chia
Anonymous
"Redhead Jen" Cassidy
Lia Eastep
The Ochenas Clan
Freckled Jenn
Jane "Ma" Powhida
Heather
Dana Russell
Allen
Karen Booker
AJ Wangler
Eric Graef
Jim Koepnick
Michele
Susie
Tony Auseon
Con Toscidis
Tom Lynch
Miss Sally's Sister
Kit
Terry & Rinn Jones

Keegan Morrow

Table of Contents

Introduction 10
An Explanation of What's to Come 10
Where Did HolyJuan Come From? 12
"I Love Me. Who Do You Love?" Explained 13
Weed Tea 15
How To Throw a Kick Ass Wedding Reception (Or: Crap that Shouldn't Be Happening at a Wedding Reception) 17
Jamole from Uganda 20
Things I Have Learned as a Husband 22
Noah's Greatest Challenge 24
How Not to Get Laid 24
Tips for Meeting Your Future Self 26
Church Wine 28
Unemployed Stuff to Do List 31
Tips for Guys Who Are Having Trouble Picking Up Girls 32
Jesus Makes Toast 34
The Last Bolt 34
The Perfect Job 37
It's Vinyl, You Wouldn't Understand 38
Phrases Women Use and Phrases Women Don't Use 39
Secret Identity Drawbacks 41
What No One Tells You About Moving 44
Jesus Emerges From the Tomb 47
Boots 48
Your Relationship as Defined by Sesame Street Characters 50
How to Fabricate Your Own Bible 52
Jesus Reads the Bible 54
Half Tie, Beer Leg... Two Tales of Friction 55

Is Sex for 30 Days Straight a Good Idea?	56
Cheaper Alternative for Gasoline	58
Ten Things Parents Will Never Admit	59
My First Beer Bong	61
Seven Things You Can Do to Help Your Relationship	63
Nuns Know	65
0 - 1 - 3 - 1 - 0 Theory	65
Parental Myths That No Parent Will Tell You About	67
What Are You Thinking About Honey?	68
How to Know When a Relationship is Over	69
Picasso and Pictionary	71
Flight Risk Apartment Mate Advice	71
Grocery Store Stereotypist	73
Jesus In a Water Balloon Fight	76
The Container and The Contents	76
An Oil Cap	79
The Secret Meaning of Road Signs	81
How to Look Busy at Work	86
Jesus at Christmas	88
Lonely on Valentine's Day	88
75 Year Old Seeks to Sell House	90
Awesome Things to Keep In Your Car Trunk	92
Jesus at the Summer Olympics	93
College Pranks	94
How to Answer a Child's Questions About Death	97
Jesus in the Shower	99
10 Phone Numbers to Sneak Into Your Friend's Phone	100
Vacuum	101
How to Tell if a Woman is Crazy	102
Jesus Plays Ball	104

Jesse Jackson is Human	104
Neighbors Park on Our Side of the Street	107
Jesus' Gym	108
Numbers and Time: A Child's View	109
Morning Math	111
How to Leave a Party Early	111
Reasons Why The Idiot In Front of You Can't Drive	112
Ikalvery	115
I Got My Hair Cut at the Black Barber Shop	116
Jesus' Shadow	118
How to Show Up Late to Work, Leave Early and Get Away With It	119
Where Thunder Comes From	121
Five Worst Types of Wingman/Wingwoman	122
You Suck, Joe Show	125
Jesus As A Child	128
How to Build a Mancave?	129
How to Hide Your Pregnancy	131
How to Make It Look Like You Are Cool for Cheap	133
If Jesus was a Woman	134
Free*	135
How To Sleep in Chicago	137
Dear HolyJuan: Can I remain friends with a Trump voter?	140
Jackson Pollock Venn Diagram	141
Phrases a Man Does Not Want to Hear from a Woman	142
The Fight that Never Was	144
Ten Reasons Why I am a Better Parent Than You	146
My Glasses	147
REAL College Essentials	149
The Lumberjack	150
How I Make Comics	151

Life Should Be More Like T-Ball 152
Panties Just Don't Do It For Me Anymore 153
The REAL 13 Things Your Pizza Guy Won't Tell You 154
Get Over Her 155
What is Up with Bread Pudding? 155
Things That Are Gone That I Miss 157
I Had A Vasectomy Today 159
RollerCoaster Tycoon Life Lessons 161
Camel Through the Eye of a Needle 162
The Friend Tiers 163
10 Ways to Pretend that you are Straight 164
Hole Story 166
Wheel of Fortune Interview 169
The End of HolyJuan? 170

Introduction

In 2006 I began writing a blog because Lia told me I should and also because I had just uninstalled the game "World of Warcraft" from my computer and didn't have anything better to do for the rest of my life.

For those of you that are unaware, a blog was something out of the early 2000s where people (usually your co-worker) could post their words and photos on the internet. No one wanted to read those words or see those photos, but it gave the bloggers a sense of accomplishment and a place to talk about how much they were under appreciated by their co-workers. Most bloggers created two posts before giving up. Over ten years, I created 1500+ posts under the name of HolyJuan. A collection of those essays, articles, comics, lists and lies are contained in this book.

Over the years, I gathered a small following. These people shared my articles and sent in "Ask HolyJuan" questions and left memorable comments. As my writing medium changed from a blog to Twitter, some of those faithful came along for the ride, and I appreciate those dedicated followers and those of you who are reading these words now.

An Explanation of What's to Come

This book contains collections, ask HolyJuan letters, how to articles, lists and comics throughout.

Collections
These stories do not require any heavy mental lifting. They are all self-contained and the reader does not need any to know any advance information to absorb the stories. Most of the names or the nicknames of the people are real, except when noted. I have made an attempt to put them in some kind of chronological order according to when they happened in my life, but many of them are stories about stories and time starts to get tricky when that happens.

Ask HolyJuan
After gaining some popularity, readers of HolyJuan.com began to email questions to me for my sage advice. I would craft responses that were more for my other readers than actual good advice for the question asking schmoes. The articles are written with the emailed question first and my response following.

How To
Many HolyJuan stories start with a single idea or shortcut that I thought was clever. I like to think that I am a pretty clever boy and that there is always more than one way to cut sandwich or convince people that a woman is not pregnant when she is trying to hide it. Some of the "How To" articles are complete bullshit while others are very thoughtful and possibly even useful to the sandwich cutting pregnant woman. I leave the usability of these stories up to the reader.

Lists
I have found that lists are a great way to get information across to readers who really do not have the time to put thought into the topic. Sometimes my lists are just a series of words, but usually they are a list with an explanation for each item. The lists sometimes cross the line into "How To" articles, but I like to play fast and loose with the facts and rules and you are a forgiving reader.

Comics
I am a horrible artist, but I love to draw cartoons. A cartoon can say in one panel what a 1000 word essay cannot. Many of my cartoons were about Jesus and I've included many of them in this book. When Jesus is in comic form, he's just too cute to be offensive, especially when he is Jesus as a Child. I've also created a "How To" article of how I make my comics using ink, paper and Photoshop.

But to start things off, I'm going to tell you were the name HolyJuan came from as well as the tile of the book, "I Love Me. Who Do You Love?"

Where Did HolyJuan Come From?

The name "HolyJuan" originally comes from playing the Ultima series games on our Apple IIc computer when I was a teenager. Players have the opportunity to name their characters and I called my different classes of characters punny names. The Ranger was "Bo Narrow," the Fighter was "Axe Anova" and the Paladin was "Holy Juan." The name of Holy Juan went to bed around 1991 when I discovered girls and alcohol. The name would have been forgotten except that I am forgetful*. (You can read that sentence four times and not understand it, but I would suggest reading onward and I'll spell it out… literally.)

Me sitting at our Apple IIc playing Ultima IV circa 1986

Around 2002, Chris Acton asked me to join a website called KungFoo.com. It was a internet discussion board and news link aggregate website. There were very fun topical discussions and endless opportunity for debate and nonsense. I joined up with the user name "Frankkenstien," which was my go to internet name at the time. I really liked KungFoo and found myself getting into fun and antagonistic debates immediately.

Screen capture from KungFoo.com circa 2006

After about a week, I forgot my password. (I am f o r g e t f u l) Instead of trying to track it down (and because I probably used a fake email address to sign up,) I created a new account using the name HolyJuan. HolyJuan became a common guest on KungFoo and several other online sites. In 2006, when I wanted to start publishing my writings online, HolyJuan was a known entity and so I stuck with it. And now you are stuck with it, too.

"I Love Me. Who Do You Love?" Explained

I didn't come up with that phrase. It's borrowed. But technically, I've lived it long enough that I could take possession because of eminent domain or squatters rights. Something like that. Here's how I learned it:

Dana is Miss Sally's good friend. She was the "maid" of honor at our wedding. (I love that the quotation marks around "maid" will give Dana a good laugh and me a punch in the arm the next time I see her. I'm highlighting this part of the book when I give her a copy.)

Dana was dating Lincoln. No, a guy named Lincoln. Lincoln was a good guy and he was helping Dana's grandfather move furniture out of his house. Load after load, Lincoln carried Grandpa Sofranko's stuff to the truck and with every load, Grandpa would stop Lincoln as he was walking out of the house and tell him a story about each item, pointing out about how that chest of drawers was hand crafted or this lamp was a family heirloom or that incredibly heavy chest was over 100 years old.

Lincoln patiently listened to each story, really just wanting to be done with the move. And just when he was about through with all of Grandpa's stories, Grandpa Sofranko put his arm around Lincoln and said, "I love me. Who do you love?"

Lincoln is no longer the boyfriend and sadly, Grandpa Sofranko is no longer with us. But his phase lives on as my mantra, "I love me. Who do you love?"

On the surface, it's a very selfish statement. But for me, it means more. Possibly because I had the chance to meet Grandpa Sofranko and knew he was a man of honor and humor. But more than likely it is because I get it. I get that being able to love yourself is the first step in being able to truly love others. I believe that it's OK for me to think that I know more than you when it comes to what I think is funny or clever. I think I can relate a funny quip or joke and then absorb the laugher from a group or singled out target. I know it is ok to say it out loud and believe it. So much so that I'd put it on the cover of a book.

I do love me. But I also hate me at times. I regret. I wish I had done differently. I know I will fail again. I fear for tomorrow. I have anxiety about my children as they have to lean in to that unforgiving world. I doubt. Doubt is the worst. Doubt makes you hesitate. Stand still. Fear. Rot.

And then I remember that I love me. I love me because I am surrounded by people who also love me. Who are willing to listen to these same stories again and again. And buy my book and come to my plays and stay married to me and love me unconditionally. I love me.

Who do you love?

Collection
Weed Tea

When I was a young teenager, my older brother and I decided to smoke the dried, tubular, hollowed out weeds that formed from the plants that grew near the creek in our back yard. We'd sneak some matches, go way into the back yard and pluck a nice fat, dried weed and break it down to a cigar sized length. We would light blue tip matches off of the dry rocks and attempt to fire up the hollow weeds. The weed really didn't light and we would end up inhaling more blue tip match sulfur than dry reed smoke.

My brother got a completely logical idea that we should use the hollow weeds as a medium to smoke something else. Like smoking something out of a wooden tube. Since we did not have any tobacco in the house or within the three-mile-radius of desolation and farms surrounding our home, we opted for the next best and obvious thing: tea.

We went in the house, opened up four Lipton tea bags and dumped the contents into a plastic sandwich bag. We disposed of the external tea bag material, string and paper by stuffing it way in the bottom of the trash can because my brother was sure mom or dad would figure out what we were up to if they found the remnants.

In the back yard, we stuffed the hollow reeds with some of the tea. We used smaller weeds to pack the tea in cannon ball style. We fired them up. He coughed. I choked. He wheezed. I hacked. Our eyes dripped tears. It was very smooth.

When we finished (probably fifteen seconds after we started) we went back inside and most likely played Atari. He probably won and he probably punched me in the arm because that's how it always was.

Three years later I was in the living room (probably playing Atari) when my mother called to me from the kitchen. I entered. Dad was sitting at the kitchen table. Mom was standing. Between them at the table was a plastic sandwich bag filled with three year old tea.

Mom did the talking. "Is this yours?"

My mind raced back. Three years ago, I had tossing that plastic bag of tea in my underwear drawer, way in the back. I'd see it every so often, but didn't think much of it as it was only tea. I never threw it away. Mom had been going through my drawers, diligently looking for weed, and low and behold she hit the mother lode.

I answered her question, "Yes. It's tea."

"Is this marijuana?"

"No! It's tea! Tea from a tea bag!"

My parents wouldn't know weed from tea so I was in for a bit of trouble trying to explain what it was.

"You have one more chance… is this marijuana?"

"No! It's tea! Steve and I tried to smoke it years ago!"

Dad finally spoke up, "You smoked… tea?"

"Yes. Out of the weeds we found by the creek."

"The hollow ones?" Dad didn't drop his apples very far from the tree.

Mom couldn't believe that her snooping was proving fruitless. "There's only one way we can tell that this is tea."

Dad put a pan of water on the stove. I was made to sit at the table and wait forever, watching for the water to boil. He dumped the contents of the bag into the water. We all waited more. I distinctly remember Dad wafting the steam to his face and saying, "Well, it smells like tea."

Fortunately, that was all the proof they needed. The weed tea was disposed of. I was given some sort of punishment that involved not being allowed to play Atari. My recollection of this story sounds brave, but I'm sure I was whimpering and high pitched stammering and I bet I ratted out my brother in the first ten seconds of the interrogation. When he came home that night, he got three years of backlogged reprimands. His punishment was probably worse because that's how it always was.

How To
How To Throw a Kick Ass Wedding Reception (Or: Crap that Shouldn't Be Happening at a Wedding Reception)

I was going to call this Top Ten Wedding Reception Pet Peeves, but I can't stand people that have pet peeves. Instead, here is a list of ten items of which you should take note and try to avoid when planning a wedding reception. I apologize for making fun of you if you have already had your wedding reception and did one of these items. Maybe you'll do better at your next wedding.

Don't Have a Long Time Between the Service and Reception
I understand that you really wanted your service at Church X and that you couldn't have your reception anywhere but Place Y and that Photographer Z could only do the group shots after the wedding and to coordinate all those desires you have a three-hour gap between the wedding and the reception. I know that you'll be busy in that time, but your wedding guests will have absolutely nothing to do except to sit in a bar and drink. Now all of a sudden you got a reception full of people that have been angrily drinking for three hours. For your next marriage, (because there's no way that anyone who planned that bullshit will ever keep a spouse) have both the wedding and the reception at the bingo hall. (Of course, there were two months between my wedding and the reception. Guilty as charged.)

Get "The Business" Done
Once you realized that the wedding and reception should be back to back, you also need to understand that a wedding isn't a kid's birthday party where you need to spread out the activities through the whole event. In your planning, make sure you cram all that traditional crap all together in the first 30 minutes of the reception. I expect the Best Man / Maid of Honor speech to run right into the cake cutting and as you are wiping the cake off your face, you should have your first dance/dance-with-dad and then throw the bouquet. Then everyone can drink uninterrupted or leave as they see fit. Don't be a prima donna and stretch out all the fluff and have everything perfectly staged and managed. Get in, get it done, get out.

Have More Than Enough Bartenders
I am a big fan of an pen bar, but I understand that your friends are alcoholics and that a cash bar helps to slow them down. What I can't stand is when a wedding of 200 has one bar with two bartenders. If I am stuck in line with an empty glass, that means that I'll also be stuck talking with one of your spouse's relatives. You don't want me to talk to your spouse's relatives because I might let the mountain goat story slide out and I don't think the statute of limitations is up on that one, pal. A reception should have a minimum of two bartenders with one bartender for every 50 people. And while I think a cash bar is fine for wine and liquor, pony up the cash

for a keg or two so that your poor friends that could only afford to get you a box of Tide as a gift can have something to drink.

BETH EDIT: I recently went to Beth's wedding and she had a great idea. As people moved from the wedding to the reception, (the wedding and reception were back to back, see the section "Long Time Between the Service and Reception"), servers made their way into the crowd with trays of wine and beer. Everyone had a drink within five minutes. Absolutely brilliant.

Don't Use a DJ Who Isn't An Actual DJ

Don't trust your buddy with an iPod and two speakers to DJ your wedding. Hire a real DJ. But during your interview, make sure you tell them that 4/5th of their payment will be held back until after the event and possibly forfeited if they break any of the following rules:

#1 No Macarena

#2 Only ONE line dance

#3 Stick to the genres of music that will be provided to you before the event. Don't stray.

#4 NO F*CKING CONGA LINE

#5 The DJ is allowed to give their phone number out to one pre-approved guest.

#6 No props.

#7 If I see a disco ball or a single multicolor rotating light, you will be beaten with a rental folding chair. Either come with a $35,000 lighting show or don't bring anything.

#8 You get one drink when the wedding is ¾ done. You can drink any of the leftovers when the reception is over.

#9 Do you really need an assistant? You are hitting NEXT on an iPod for f*cks sake.

#10 And most of all... don't give color commentary on anything that anyone is doing. You are to speak only when announcing events as they happen. Don't tell us what song you are going to play next. Don't tell us how lovely the bride looks. Don't mention that Aunt Eleanor is really shaking it out on the dance floor with that new hip. Just keep hitting play and you'll get your check.

Release the Tables
If you can't afford the extra $15,000 to have servers bring the dry chicken and salty asparagus to your guests, you might decide to have a buffet. That's fine because your guests aren't really worth the extra money. But if you do have a buffet, don't leave it up to your guests to decide when they should stand up to go stand in line. Release the tables by number or have a couple of family members do it for you. Just don't pretend like your starving guests can regulate the line. Someone is going to ditch Aunt Elenaor and she has been pretty feisty since she got that hip replaced. I once attended a wedding where the father of the bride walked into a room with over 250 people in it and said, "The buffet line is open," and left. 250+ people looked at each other for six seconds and then stood up in unison to head towards the food. Miss Sally and I walked the f*ck out.

Don't Invite Guests to the Reception at the Last Minute
Please don't invite last minute guests that you meet through the wedding process. At a recent wedding, I asked about two of the scantily clad women who were spending a lot of time grinding on each other and several of the relatives. The reply I got was that the two girls were the strippers from the bachelor party and the groom took such a liking to them that he invited them to the reception. TRUE STORY.

Do Not Ever Do The Cake Smash
Don't smash the cake in each other's faces. And if you do, plan it out ahead of time so you both do it to each other in some fun way that will make it to YouTube so that you can generate some ad revenue and pay for the third and fourth bartender. Unless you are going to make money off of it, don't ever smash the cakes in each other's face.

Get Out There And Dance
This one has to do more with a combination of the DJ and the guests, but I clearly blame the guests for this one. Receptions must be successful. Even if the bride and groom do everything as instructed above, the reception can fail if you, the guest, don't dance. Don't make the bride pull you off your chair and on to the dance floor. Suck it up for one night and dance. If you see the dance floor is empty, tell your pals to get off their asses and at least sway out on the dance floor. This is the one opportunity for the DJ to use his "Line Dance" card. Make sure he doesn't blow it in the first ten minutes of the reception. Come on… just dance. You saw Footloose, Willard… you know how to dance.

The "Kill You" Speech
I didn't think this one was real, but I have witnessed it at three (yes, three) weddings. At some point during the bridesmaid's speech, someone, either a male family member or close female friend of the bride, will profess their love of the

bride and then say something along the lines of, "…and if you ever hurt her, I will hunt you down and kill you." Are you f*cking kidding me? You might be saying it in jest, but it makes you sound A) creepy and B) creepy. Just tell them how happy you are for them and sit down. And really, if you feel the need to say this, look at your own meaningless, empty life and try to figure out why you feel the need to say such things. There is still hope for you. Maybe.

Complainers

You are now familiar with this list and understand that some people make mistakes in the planning of their receptions. Now keep it to yourself, asshole. There is a time and a place to complain about a reception and that is the day after. Don't bitch about the DJ or the bartenders or how long shit is taking during the reception. You are a guest and you should act like one. Get off your ass and dance. Stand in the bar line and chat it up with Uncle Chris. Laugh at the DJs commentary about how the Bride and Groom will be (insert sexual innuendo here) later. No one is perfect. Especially the guy who had his reception in a bingo hall, with no DJ except for a crappy CD player, had volunteer bartenders, and will never ever, ever be allowed to help plan with his wedding reception again. At some point I will, I mean, he will have to throw a second one to make up for the first.

Collection
Jamole from Uganda

The Baskin Robbins in Lancaster, OH was located at the corner of Memorial and 6th in what I think was an old gas station. That store had huge windows that faced the crossroads and from either roadway you could look in and see the employees screwing around during all hours of the day. The guy that owned the competing ice cream store down the road once said to me, "I wouldn't be one bit surprised if I drove by and saw those kids having sex on the back counter."

We were always doing something stupid, whether it was making outrageous concoctions of coke syrup mixed with coffee and dry ice or finding clever ways to interact with the customers. The ice cream cases had vertical glass fronts that women would unknowingly mash their breasts into. Because we wore hats, I could keep my brim down as I pretended to look at the tubs of ice cream. Two scoops?

We usually kept our shenanigans to closing time on non-busy nights. People walking in the doors at 10:59pm on a Wednesday would be greeted with us wearing our aprons on our heads as we chased one another with whipped cream cans. If we got busted, there was a back room for us to go streaking into to collect ourselves. I had fun one evening when Katrina and I taped 5 gallon buckets to our feet and served customers about 20 inches taller than anyone that walked in. No one said a thing as we klonked around the store on those giant plastic buckets.

Russ, Iva, me and Dave from the LHS yearbook circa 1988

One of the more complicated stunts we pulled off was "Jamole from Uganda" (pronounced yah-MOLE.) We got out a TRAINEE badge and used the name tag maker to make Jamole's name tag. I wore my hat all the way down, like all foreign exchange students would, buttoned my shirt all the way up and tied my apron up as high as it would go. I used an accent that was mostly Indian and what I thought was African. When customers would come in, my co-worker Dave would loudly pressure me to work. Guests would rattle off their order and I would say, "Speak slow. I am Jamole from Uganda." Dave would yell, "He's not from around here!" I would make correct change, but count it back in a fake foreign language. I would purposely pick out the wrong cone and Dave would come over, slap it out of my hand and loudly correct me. "No Jamole! Sugar! Cone!" Once customers were served and sitting down, Dave would give me lessons about the United States and make me sweep the floor.

I was in the middle of the Jamole act with some customers when my buddy DT's parents walked in. I was in the school play with DT and we played football together, so I knew his parents very well. Don and Kate saddled up next to the couple I had been working over with my "make change in gibberish" routine and said, "Hi Doug! How are you?"

I said, "Gud," in my Ugandan accent.

"Are you excited for the play?"

"Jes."

The man in the other couple turned to Don's folks and said, "He doesn't speak English very well."

Luckily, Dave walked up to serve DT's parents and I streaked into the back room.

I came back out once DT's parents left. The next time I saw DT, he mentioned that his parents saw me at Baskin Robbins the other night. He said they were positive that I did not recognize them. But I did... Jamole remembers everything.

List
Things I Have Learned as a Husband

Filling a dirty pan with water and letting it soak is not considered washing it.

Staying out late is being out until 11:59 pm.
Staying out all night is anytime past 12:01 am.

If your wife says she doesn't want jewelry, she does.

Wives like sex, just not right now.

The bed does not make itself. Saying that you are just going to sleep in it again is not a valid excuse.

It was not pure luck that my work shirts are hanging in the closet.

Always keep track of favors and tasks. If you owe, it's best to remember and pay up. It is human nature to remember that you've done the laundry the last 30 times or given the last 5 baths. Try to keep it even.

My kids might have a sense of humor and know what The Force is because of me, but all the other credit goes to my wife.

Don't mention that you found hair in the shower.

Most everything is a test. I'm scoring in the low 20s and there is no curve.

Grey hair only exists on my head.

"Putting away leftovers" does not mean eating what's left out of the pan, over the sink.

Whole cucumbers do not belong in the garbage disposal no matter what cool noise they make.

If there is a good looking girl at work, I immediately go home and tell my wife about her. I'm not sure why except that it seems like the right thing to do.

It's not worth arguing about toilet seat status or how much toilet paper makes up a single use.

When you get into an argument in the car there is usually nothing interesting to look at out the window.

Whoever cooks, the other person does the dishes.

It is better for me to go to work unshaven than to use the pink razor in the shower. (Or I should learn to rinse the pink razor better.)

Don't discuss your sex life on the internet.

Before two kids it was morning sex. After two kids it's mourning sex.

I am not a very good learner.

My wife is the most tolerant woman in the world. I love her very much. Happy Valentine's Day!

(A website article is not considered a valid Valentine's Day present. Nor is reposting it in a book.)

Comic
Noah's Greatest Challenge

Ask HolyJuan
How Not to Get Laid

Dear Holy Juan~

I have a male friend who I find very interesting, but not *sleep with* interesting. But I want to go out with him because it would be fun. How can I ask him out for a drink without him thinking that I want to get laid?
~Marcie
dogsdontpurr.com

Dear Wavy Line Marcie,

I am proficient in all fields. I am an expert in several fields. In one field and one field only, I am a Master: Not Getting Laid. For this letter, your prospective non-date's name is Carl. (Sorry, Carls.)

Step One: Do not say drink in the invitation
Most the time a woman wants to get a drink, she wants to lose her ability to think reasonably and to forget how to keep her pants on. Instead, invite Carl out for lunch or early dinner. Lunch is a definite boner bender. Early dinner suggests you've got other people to bang later. I'm not saying you can't get a drink when you are out; just don't suggest it in the invite.

Step Two: Call it a meeting
Meetings suck the life out of anyone. No one gets laid at a meeting. When you invite Carl to lunch, say you want to discuss a specific topic that does not include ex-boyfriends. Architecture and retirement are great topics to keep Carl from boning up. Again, you don't have to discuss that at lunch, but it will keep Carl's expectations at a bare minimum.

Step Three: Schedule a gynecologist visit right before your meeting
You are weak and might f*ck Carl despite your attempt to con me into thinking you don't want to. As a backup, schedule a Pap or a regular gyno visit right before your meeting with Carl. This will destroy any chance of you wanting to get busy. Ensure you mention that you are late to the lunch because of the gyno appointment and, for added realism, let a speculum fall out of your purse and on to the table. Follow that up with a, "So that's where that went."

Step Four: Order wings
Wings are greasy, disgusting and delicious. A chick eating wings is hot only is she is eating them off your chest during sex. Watching you suck down twelve, greasy wings will turn Carl off. If he starts to get excited watching you lick the sauce off your fingers, remember to mention that wings give you the shits.

Step Five: Burning itch
Scratch a lot. Complain of burning while you pee. Ask Carl what has been happening in local politics since you've been overseas in Thailand.

Step Six: Dutch
Splitting the bill is the universal sign that no one is getting laid. If Carl insists on paying, wait until he hands the waiter his credit card and say your good-bye, insisting that you are about to have a blow-out from the wings tearing through your intestines. If he pays in cash and tells the waiter to keep the change, ask him in a loud voice how his counterfeiting operation is doing. Sneak out when the manager comes to the table.

Step Seven: F*ck him
Oh well. At least you gave it your best shot

How To
Tips for Meeting Your Future Self

At some point, time travel will be invented and your future self will come back to warn you about something. Be prepared by following these tips.

1. Have a secret question
Be wary of evil future selves. If it is actually your future self, they will know the answer to the secret question; something only you would know. Like where you masturbated for the first time (in a bedroom closet.) Don't make up a secret word (this can be figured out with future technology and "ditto" has been taken.) If your future self doesn't remember the secret question, kill them with the really sharp knife in your boot.

2. Always carry a sharp knife in your boot.
See #1

3. Immediately ask for the winner of the 20XX Super Bowl.
Time travel will not be cheap and the only way you are going to make enough money to travel back in time is to make a shit load of money betting on sports. That will only happen if you know the actual results of the future games. Your future self will know this and they will have a prepared list of sporting events from the future (their past.) If your future self gives you some bullshit excuse like that it is against the "laws of time travel" or that they are coming back in time to keep you from winning all that money and becoming a rich prick, kill them and analyze their blood to siphon off some futuristic antibiotic or cure-all medicines.

4. Cross your arms and give your future self a disapproving look.
It worked for my friend Erik.

Eric folds crosses his arms and stares down his future self.

5. Kill your future self
Your future self is nothing but trouble. He's all full of "doom and gloom" and "don't do this" and "don't eradicate that race of peoples." As soon as your future self answers the secret question, get the future sports questions from them and then kill them with the gun in your other boot (they will know that you keep a knife in your boot and have some sort of futuristic knife protection on.) Collect his blood for testing and then dispose of the body.

6. Always carry a gun in your boot, but forget about it so your future self won't know you have it.
(See #5.)

7. Get a shit load of insurance on yourself.
Once your future self arrives and before you kill them with the boot gun that you have forgotten about, have them over to your crappy apartment/house and while they are asleep, get a whole lot of insurance out on yourself. Get an ungodly amount of coverage and name yourself as the beneficiary (most insurance companies will completely go for this as they will think it is impossible for you to collect on your own death.) Go back and complete step #5 (except for the dispose

of the body) and collect the money for your own death. And don't let the insurance company claim that it was suicide because you killed yourself.

8. On second thought, kill your future self immediately
Use the grenade you have in your back pocket that you must forget about because you can't seem to forget the gun and the knife and your future self is wearing a bullet proof vest with futuristic knife proof clothing.

9. (I was kidding about the grenade... make it a crossbow)
See #8. Your future self will plan for the grenade and you can surprise them with the crossbow. REALLY...FORGET ABOUT THE CROSSBOW NOW to trick your future self!

10. Plan ahead
Forget you read this so that the future you will be completely unprepared. As a matter of fact, tear the pages out of this book.

Collection
Church Wine

As a kid raised in a Catholic family, we sometimes got to sit up on the altar during mass. All the families rotated through. It was a great time for mom to practice pinching four children simultaneously to keep us from wiggling, nudging, squirming and what boiled down to dicking around up there in plain view of 200 or so judgmental people. The view from the altar is much better than from the pews. More people to look at. You can see the nails in Jesus up close. See the priest from the backside. (Insert your own Catholic priest joke here.)

It was the job of the family on the altar to help out during the service, like to present the gifts to the priest during mass and clean up when he is done. The gifts are the sacramental bread and wine that represent Jesus after he died, quit drinking and went gluten free. Before mass, the priest would prepare the wine and wafers in the priest green room and the family would sneak them out to the altar before mass started.

In the secret lair of the priest, the wine was stored in a locked cabinet. The key to the cabinet was on a woven, purple string. It was probably just a piece of string or something simple, but it seemed special. The priest would need to get the wine and pour it in a golden chalice for transportation to the stage... err, altar. Church wine was special. I knew it was special because it came in a small, odd shaped bottle with letters and numbers on it. There was also a picture of grapes on it in case anyone needed to be reminded that it was wine. When he opened the locked cabinet, I saw that bottle and it was burned into my memory. In my mind, I could see the priests that worked in the wine fields, picking those same illustrated grapes, stomping on them, putting the liquid in barrels with God smiling from above. In time, the holy liquid would be bottled in those very special bottles and shipped to churches across the world.

Back in the priest's lair, it was poured in a chalice, the bottle recapped and locked back in the cabinet.

When you are twelve and Catholic, you get a sip of wine during communion. My brother would dare me to take a gulp, but God would get pissed, and I was already in trouble with him for the constant masturbation.

At the end of communion, the priest would drink any leftover wine. I remember thinking that being a priest has its perks!

Everyone would leave the church and the priest would shake hands and say goodbye. While that was going on, the family would help to clean up. The priest would say thanks and be thankful that our family wouldn't be back on rotation for another 18 months.

Flash forward to years later. I'm no longer twelve, but I am not yet twenty-one. I am in the backseat of a car that is going through a drive-thru to illegally buy beer. (Ohio has actual drive-thru beer stores. Cars drive into the building; the guy who sells the beer sucks down exhaust, checks the fake IDs, takes the wrinkled cash and then the cars drive out.) My buddy Doob is in the front seat, questioning the guy about the different kinds of beers. We are all silently yelling at him to shut up, order a 24 pack of Old Milwaukee and move on. Trying to look busy not looking at the beer guy, I pretended to take interest in the other beers right outside my window in the glass coolers.

Church wine. Church wine! They had church wine at the beer drive-thru!

I turned to Russ. "Hey, they have church wine here."

Russ didn't know what I was talking about. "What are you talking about?"

I pointed. That wine. "The one with the numbers and letters. And the grapes!! It's church wine. It's a special Catholic Church wine."

"You mean the Mad Dog?"

I had heard of Mad Dog. It was like liquor or something. "No. The one with MD and 20/20. That's church wine."

The car was now pulling away. Doob was somehow able to buy the beer and not get busted. Russ said, "The one with the MD is Mad Dog. MD. Mad Dog. It's fortified wine. It's what bums drink because it's cheap."

My whole life was a sham. The special wine. The locked cabinet. The priests in the field. God smiling down as the bottles were shipped around the world. It was all one big lie. One oddly shaped bottle with screw top cap, numbers and letter and a picture of grapes lie.

It's been a long time since I have had church wine. I remember the taste. The dare to take a chug. The special bottle with the M and D. Numbers. And a picture of beautiful, plump grapes. And still wishing it was magical.

List
Unemployed Stuff to Do List

Unemployed Stuff to do list.

1. ~~MAKE LIST~~
2. ✓ CROSS OFF ITEM #1
3. ✓ STEAL STENO PAD FROM OLD JOB
4.
5. BRAINSTORM TO CREATE A #4 TASK
6. ✓✓✓✓✓✓✓ SURF THE NET
7. ✓ TELL THE WIFE I SENT OUT 10 RESUMES
8. ✓ POST "UNEMPLOYED STUFF TO DO LIST" ON THE INTERNET

www.holyjuan.com

List/How To (Some of these are combos. Consider it a bonus.)
Tips for Guys Who Are Having Trouble Picking Up Girls

If you are a guy and having problems picking up girls, please allow me to help you. I have over 27 years of past experience not being able to pick up girls. I then employed several of these methods and got myself a real catch. Here's what you need to do:

Dump your current friends
If you aren't able to pick up girls, it probably has to do with the company you keep. I feel the best method for meeting girls is to utilize a friend to be the good cop or the bad cop. If your current friends are as hopeless as you or they don't have the time to help you out because they already have a girl, get rid of them. What you really need is a Handsome Joe as a friend. He'll play the good cop to your bad cop. He'll like the blonde so you can have the brunette. The beer commercials call him your wingman. I call him the Handsome Joe. Get rid of your Brian or John and get yourself a Handsome Joe.

Move
You probably can't pick up girls because you are stuck in a horrible rut or in Lorain, Ohio. The same bars. The same social scene. You are the fan of the same local sports team that everyone else is. You are scared to change your home turf because you'd have to lie to be different and you have enough trouble being confident in your sorry self. So pack up and get out. Move somewhere else and be yourself. In a different town, you'll stand out because you like stuff from your old town and you will seem foreign and romantic. You'll order a hoagie and girls at the sub shop will think you are speaking French. (Chicks dig French.) You'll go to the sports bar in "Team B" jersey and girls who grew up with "Team A" will think you are a bad boy. If all else fails, you can move back home and bring some essence from the last town back home with you. Tell harrowing stories of how you stood up for "Team B" and ate foreign food and took public transportation.

Learn French
Chicks dig French. You don't have to learn the whole language or verb tenses. Just pick up 50–60 words and learn the accent. Mix in a few real French words with French inflections on American words and you'll be set. If you run into a girl who does speak French, pretend you are from Serbia and that you are just learning English and French. Then fake a groin pull and get out of there. (Excusez-moi, j'ont tiré mon aine. Je devrai partir maintenant. Merci.)

Wash your clothes in baby detergent
I know this sounds completely f'd up, but stick with me. It is a well-known fact that all women love babies. Babies tend to have a certain smell about them that when it isn't poop or breast milk breath, is the crazy scent they put into the baby laundry detergent. These marketing folks started adding a scent into baby detergent years ago and all humans have evolved into believing that babies actually smell that way. With a hint of baby underneath your suggestion of cologne, women will be unknowingly drawn to you. Somehow you'll have a reproductive edge about you and women will want to sleep with you. Now, if you do get called out on the smell, make sure you make an excuse like you are watching your sister's kids while she has stomach cancer surgery and that was the only detergent she had. Pull a groin. Get out.

Become a bartender
There are several bartending schools in any given town. Take the six week course. Get a job at any bar. No matter what, you will get laid. Don't be picky. Most bartenders are not. The cool guys will take the good ones during the night. You will get the drunk ones that you have been over-pouring for the last four hours. In the morning, if she doesn't run screaming from your apartment, maybe she'll go to breakfast with you and not give you a fake number. Either way, you'll get to go into work the next night and try again.

Smoke or pretend like you do
Dirty girls smoke. Girls that smoke like it when a guy can offer them a cigarette or a light for their pre-existing cigarette. If you do not have an opening line, offer a cigarette. Then a light. Then talk about how the new smoking laws stink or that cigarette tax is too high. This will lead to other branches of conversation. Maybe she'll bring up how smokers feel alone and you'll now have something in common.

So keep a pack of cigarettes on you. It is best to have 100s in two of the major brands. If the girl is smoking Virginia Slims or Capris – STAY AWAY.

Bonus! It is also a well-known fact that if a girl will put a cigarette in her mouth, she'll put anything in her mouth.

Date a woman with kids
Sometimes your only option is the final option.

Comic
Jesus Makes Toast

Collection
The Last Bolt

The summer break before my junior year of college had me living at home: roofing during the weekdays and going out just about every night. On this particular Saturday morning, I woke up from four hours of sleep with a bit of a hangover. Dad was calling for me to get dressed and ready to go. Sitting mostly up in bed, I remembered that Dad's 1987 Reliant wagon had broken down on the 270 outerbelt in Columbus and we needed to go up and fix it. I was needed as monkey boy and to drive the second car back.

As we drove up to Columbus, Dad explained that the alternator had been going out and it finally gave up on his way home from work on Friday afternoon. After he got ahold of mom to pick him up, he called the Columbus City Police to tell them he'd be back up the next morning to get the station wagon. They said they would not tow it.

To get to the station wagon, we had to drive past it on the opposite side of the outerbelt and loop back around at an overpass. We overpassed, took the on ramp and about half a mile later we parked and got the tools out. I stood around and half listened as Dad spoke of car engines in Korea and how back in World War 2 "the Japanese were awful bastards" and "they were smaller and would shoot you in the knees." It was then that the family curse snuck up on us. There were four bolts that held the alternator in place. Three of the bolts came out just fine, but The Last Bolt was stuck. It was always the last bolt. Dad applied force and more force. He Liquid Wrenched and tapped. He bruised the back of his hands and split his knuckles open. He pleaded and cursed. He went so far as to have me try to remove it. The last bolt was stuck. So we stood on the side of the road, taking turns at giving it one more try with dad lamenting, "Why does it always have to be The Last Bolt?"

And then, with a crack, Dad freed the stubborn last bolt.

And in that split second, the world was good and everything was going to be all right. He pulled the alternator out and left all the tools and car parts scattered throughout the engine compartment.

We took the part to a dealership and Dad asked how much a replacement would be. He laughed at the lady though the window, "You've got to be kidding?" The dealership cost was four times what it cost at the parts store in Lancaster. Dad was outraged! Dad was also not in a place to bargain. He paid for it and we left. In the car he said that he would install the new alternator, go back to Lancaster and buy a cheaper replacement and then return the expensive one back to the dealership. Clever!

As we drove past the broken down car for the second time that day, we couldn't help but notice that the car's front end was elevated and attached to a City of Columbus tow truck. Dad tried to roll down the window and yell, "No! No! No!" but at 65 mph it was impossible. We zoomed up and over the exit with dad's incredulous mutterings filling the car with rage. By the time we reached the spot, all of the tow truck and most the station wagon were gone. We had left the nuts, bolts and tools sitting top of the engine and some escaped through the bottom of the engine with the help of gravity when the tow truck pulled away. The parts lie there on the side of the road like a police outline of a dead body. The others were probably leaving a trail, like bread crumbs, around 270 and to the impound lot.

Dad was so enraged that he could not speak or yell. I didn't say anything for fear of giving his anger purchase. Without a word, he drove to a phone booth and called the police. They said there was nothing they could do, pick your car up from the impound lot and have a nice day.

We drove to the impound lot and paid for the car's release and several additional fees. Dad mentioned that we needed to put a part in the car and the lady said that no work was allowed to be done on the lot and that we would have to pay to have the car towed off the lot and to the side of the road. Dad said, "Oh… no thanks. We'll just drive it off and repair it." As we walked out, I said that the car wouldn't start without repairing it. Dad flatly smiled, "We'll see about that."

Dad marched alone into the lot with a wrench and the new alternator, his pockets clunking with the escaped nuts and bolts.

And somehow, in less than eight minutes, he drove the mostly functional station wagon out of the lot and to the side of the road. By some means, using the remaining parts and tools that had remained in cracks and crevices of the engine, he got the alternator partially installed, slapped on the belt and tightened it enough to get out of the lot.

He spent a few minutes tightening the existing bolts and re-adjusting the belt. "That will be enough to get us home. Follow me." And then we drove off separately together.

The moral of this story is that there really is no Last Bolt. The Last Bolt is really the most difficult thing that is put off until last. In life, it is easier to do the easy thing first and then complain about the hard thing.

Ask HolyJuan
The Perfect Job

Dear Holy Juan,
You seem to be all knowing, so tell me, how can I find the perfect job that pays great, the people are friendly, office politics don't exist, the commute is short, the hours are 10 to 5p and the dress code is casual?

Thanks for your insight!

Desperately Seeking Employment

Dear Desperately Seeking Employment,

First off, let me console you on the loss of your job at the Baby Seal Fur Processing Facility #23. I know you started as a humble Club Duller and worked your way up to Club Duller 3.

It's tough finding the PERFECT job. But I can help you. Let's look at you "perfect" job specifics:

1. Pays Great
I assume you will want to make $100,000 plus a year.

2. Friendly People
This is impossible, so you will need to work alone or have your personality removed.

3. No office politics
Again, work alone.

4. Short commute
A short commute to me means about 45 – 60 seconds.

5. Hours are 10-5
A seven-hour work day? Don't kid yourself. Most people only get in 4–5 hours of office face time and two of that is lunch and coffee breaks. Subtract internet surfing and most people work about 30 minutes a day. Well mark you down from 2:00pm – 2:30pm.

6. Casual Dress Code
To me, casual is nude.

OK. Let's throw all these variables into the HolyJuan Career-o-Matic and see what it spits out.

(chink-a-chink-a-chink-a-chink)

YOUR CAREER **BLOGGER**

Awesome! That's my career too!

Good luck with that and let me know if there is anything else I can help you with.

Comic
It's Vinyl, You Wouldn't Understand

List
Phrases Women Use and Phrases Women <u>Don't</u> Use

My friend Stephanie likes to send me e-mails to remind me that I, as a male, am a simpleton and should just listen without provocation to what any woman says. Here is the list she sent me:

Phrases Women Use

<u>Fine</u>: This is the word women use to end an argument when they are right and you need to shut up.

<u>Five minutes</u>: If she is getting dressed, this means a half-an-hour. Five minutes is only five minutes if you have just been given five more minutes to watch the game before helping around the house.

<u>Nothing</u>: This is the calm before the storm. This means "something," and you should be on your toes. Arguments that begin with "nothing" usually end in "fine."

<u>Go ahead</u>: This is a dare, not permission. Don't Do It!

<u>Loud sigh</u>: This is actually a word, but is a non-verbal statement often misunderstood by men. A loud sigh means she thinks you are an idiot and wonders why she is wasting her time standing here and arguing with you about nothing. (Refer back to #3 for the meaning of nothing.)

<u>That's okay</u>: This is one of the most dangerous statements a women can make to a man. That's okay means she wants to think long and hard before deciding how and when you will pay for your mistake.

<u>Thanks</u>: A woman is thanking you, do not question, or Faint. Just say you're welcome.

<u>Whatever</u>: Is a women's way of saying F**K YOU!

<u>Don't worry about it, I got it</u>: Another dangerous statement, meaning this is something that a woman has told a man to do several times, but is now doing it herself. This will later result in a man asking "What's wrong?" For the woman's response refer to #3.

I would follow that list up with the following:

Phrases Women Don't Use

<u>Yes you can</u>: Women will never say this. Ever. Unless the man asks if he can give her a foot massage or shove his head up his own ass.

<u>No thanks, one scoop is enough</u>: Obvious. Works with most portions like slice, bowl or dozen.

<u>I don't understand</u>: Women will instead say, "I understand" even if they don't just so they don't look like they are stupid. When the thing they don't understand catches on fire, then they ask for help by screaming.

<u>Would you like to have sex again?</u>: More obvious.

<u>I like your friends</u>: You won't hear this unless she is hooking up with one of them.

<u>I'll buy</u>: You might hear this one, but she really doesn't mean it. Get out your wallet, champ.

<u>I'll change the tire</u>: It's not that they don't know how to, it's just that their jeans are so low that if they bend over they might misplace the tire iron down their crack. What they don't realize is that just by bending over on the side of the road, 8–10 cars, Harleys and semis will stop and ask if she needs help.

<u>This makes my ass look big</u>: You might think you have heard this one before, but as a question in the form of "DOES this make my ass look big." Your response to either was probably the same and you are still not going to get any action.

<u>Can my friend join in?</u>: You'll never hear this one. Unless the friend is a dude and your role is to hold the camera.

Ask HolyJuan
Secret Identity Drawbacks

Dear Holy Juan,

Life is getting complicated, so I am thinking about creating my own secret identity. What are the unexpected drawbacks to having an alter ego?

Thanks,
Dwight Story

Dear Mr. Story,

You've come to the right place. This may be the first ever Ask HolyJuan question that I am certified to answer. Of course, I came from this backwards, though it was forwards for me; my life was not complicated and developing alter ego(s) made it extremely complicated.

When one develops a secret alter ego online, you go through several phases and run into several complications. But first, let me give you a few tips:

Tip #1: Don't do it
Just stop now. Keep your life at this level of complication. You won't regret it.

Tip #2: A secret one person can't keep
You didn't listen to Tip #1, so let's work on keeping this thing anonymous. Your greatest enemy is yourself, because once you do create an anonymous identity, you will want to tell one other person. Don't. They will tell one other person and so on and the next thing you know, your mother will be calling you asking who this alter ego is. So if you can keep it to yourself, that's a good start.

Tip #3: A secret identity means secret everything
The internet is a nosey sonofabitch. It wants to know your email address, cell phone number, your contacts, Twitter user name, Facebook friends and LinkedIn connections. And by having just one of those things, it can look at other people on the internet and see who has that information in their Contacts (because some people are silly enough to share their contacts with a website or app.) Once it makes a connection, it will then try to get people to connect with you, including coworkers, classmates, enemies, and exes. To combat this, you need to create a whole new identity and not just a random user name. Start with Gmail and create a new email address that is a series of random letters and numbers. Go to Google Voice and get a phone number. Now, do it all again, this time with a new set of

random letters and new Google voice number. You now have two emails and two phone numbers that you can cross reference against each other when a website asks for an email, backup email or phone number. You will only use these emails to create the new alter ego. (I mentioned this was complicated, remember?)

Tip #4: Pick your new identity
Your new identity or username will want to be something that has nothing to do with who you are now and who you want people to assume you are. I like to mix a tile with a number, a Wes Anderson character and a body part in some random order. Examples include:
MrTwelveKumarElbow
DrCaptainSharpPancreasTwentySeven
MrsNineteenRoyalLiver
Don't write your number as a number, as it will look like a spam account and that defeats the purpose of getting people to wonder who you are.

Tip #5: One device only
Only access your alter ego from one device that is solely used for that purpose. If you are constantly logging in and logging off different accounts from the same device or computer, at some point you are going to screw up and post something real to the anonymous account or vice versa. Then people will be able to cross reference that with the real you and you'll be screwed.

You've created your alter ego and it is private, secure and no one will know who you are. What's next? The four phases of anonymity, of course.

1. Elation
Freedom at last! Say what you want without fear of retribution. Admit faults. Confess your sins. Out yourself. Write a blog with your real feelings about religion and politics. Revel in the joy that is freedom from persecution of what you say from the people in your real life.

2. Loneliness
Soon, that euphoria passes. When you are admitting your faults or opinions to other people that you don't know you, there is no long lasting joy in spouting off to a revolving door of people who don't care what you say or don't have interest in someone who is obviously hiding their identity. You can't post photos of yourself, because the people you piss off in the next phase will do a reverse image search and track you down. Any of that elation is probably gone.

3. Boredom

Soon, you will run out of sins to share. People don't like to have real conversations with fake people, they will say not nice things. Because you are anonymous, you can also say not nice things back. Instead of finding a creative way to argue with someone, you will take the easy insult out. It will become boring very quickly. The worst part is that you begin to let this attitude sneak into your real interactions. You will begin to find it difficult to turn off your fake personality because it isn't your fake personality, it was you all along. Soon you realize that the real you is the fake you and the alter ego is just you hiding behind that MrsPagodaEightBrain username. At some point, you will make the jump to the last phase.

4. Reveal

You decide to come out of the closet and let one very close friend know that you are that anonymous person. They check out some of what you said and they are… not surprised. They don't see anything wrong with the things you are saying and are still your friend. You finally have this weight of things you secretly said off your chest and the world is good again. You give your friend a big hug and send them out the door. Of course, they will text someone ten seconds later and let them know. Once the cat is out of the bag, you can write a book about it and put that information as an attribute in your LinkedIn profile. At least that's what I did. When I search the internet for "HolyJuan," there are some nasty things that I said to people when I was truly anonymous. But I also think I said some interesting, humorous and silly things.

In conclusion, Dwight Story (or is it MsMrFoxOneToe?), I highly suggest an alter ego to kick off your journey to self-awareness. And maybe you, unlike me, will be able to succeed in keeping your secret identity secret. If it makes you happy and serves to make your life less complicated, go for it. Just please let me know your fake name. I promise I won't tell. Promise.

Yours truly,
DrChasTenenbaumIntestinesThree

How To
What No One Tells You About Moving

Moving is highly underrated: both in time and treasure. I've helped several friends to move and here's what I've noticed that you should consider before moving.

0.5 The PLAN
(It's best to have the PLAN in the #0.5 spot so that you can sneak up on the #1 item.)
Create a PLAN for the move. Write it down. Stick to it. Even if you are wrong, because once people begin to doubt you, they'll start to argue and that is a time suck. Be willing to take advice, but don't let anyone tell you what to do. This is why you do not invite your dad to the move.

1. Packing takes 20% longer than expected
OK, you've heard this before, but no matter how you plan, packing will take 20% longer. Even after you read this, you might think, "I'll just increase the time by 20%." Wrong. Because it will take 20% longer than that. It's a losing proposition. It is in your best interest to schedule five hours to pack so that it will only take six. (And don't think you can plan on five minutes of moving so that it will take six. Fate is not stupid.)

2. Pack everything
Put as much as you can in boxes. It makes packing the truck so much easier. Leave stuff in drawers if you want, but make sure you cover with cardboard and tape. Take this opportunity to throw out all your lamps. They are hard to pack and just not worth your time. DO NOT PACK THINGS IN SUITCASES. It is a well-known fact that suitcases are the number one item that get lost both at the airport and in a move.

3. Don't pack everything
Screw that last bit. Take the time to get rid of stuff. Have your friends take stuff. Call the local charity that will haul it away. Put it on the curb so the local junk-truck-guy can come by and take the good stuff. Especially those lamps.

4. Color code
In the end, you will be much happier will all your crap in well-marked, color coded boxes You can write the details of the box in small letters, but use large words or color to help guide the unpackers to the room they need to go. The night before the move, go to the new house and make signs with arrows. Color code rooms and doors. This will alleviate you standing at the front door of the new house, blocking the door deciding what the hell you were thinking last night when you wrote KT BT 9 FR on the box.

5. Rent the bigger truck
Rent the biggest truck you can get your hands on. Find a friend with a commercial driver's license if you have to. Two trips SUCKS. Spend the extra money because you will save it in the end with mileage and time.

6. You can have too many people to help
It's easy to understand that if you are the only one moving your furniture, you are screwed. But is it possible to have too many people? YES. One of my favorite economics terms is "diminishing returns." It basically means that the more people you throw at a job, at some point, the amount of work that can get done is reduced. When you have too many people standing around, they will have the time to stop and criticize your PLAN. If you invite too many people to help, divide them up into smaller teams for continued packing, labeling, cleaning, lifting or send some over to the new place to get rid of them. Have them buy the beer and put it into the new refrigerator. Part of your PLAN should be a list of things for the ne'er-do-wells to do while the real help is doing their job.

7. Inside help / outside help
Your job during the move is to coordinate. Try not to get stuck moving anything. You should be able to freely move in and out of the house. If you have the person power, have someone in the house, who is familiar with the PLAN, that can guide the movers or get you in a hurry if there is a question. You can then be near the truck to help with loading, unless you suck at Tetris.

8. Tight pack
If you are crappy at Tetris, I would suggest getting a friend who has move experience to pack the truck. You want a tight pack as this means less damage and more stuff on the truck. Have room outside the truck for staging items that should go on later or when you have a futon-shaped hole to fill.

9. MOVE EVERYTHING NOW
Damnit! I've seen it a hundred times. Towards the end of the move, little stuff is still lying around the house and the owner will say, "I'll get that stuff later." Don't do it. MOVE IT NOW. You've got the people and the truck. For fragile stuff also have a fleet of cars that will be going to the new house. Just do it now. If you are moving across the country, you might want to keep personal items or papers with you, just don't overthink it, champ. Move it now.

10. Don't feed in the middle of a move
Hungry people work harder. Full people nap. Don't schedule your move around a meal time. Wait until the move is over to order the pizza. Even if it is late. By then, people will be sick of you and they will leave so you can order less pizza. Only keep cold water at the house you are moving out of. Make sure that beer is only at the new place so they have a goal. Drunk people drop shit and argue with you.

11. Don't get fancy

Provide water. Provide pizza. Provide beer. Don't try and cater. Don't even think about cooking out. Your friends knew this when they volunteered to help. They will move someday and you will get the same crap from them.

12. Unpack now

If you do not unpack a box, it will remain packed until you move again. This falls in line with Move Everything Now. People are there. Unpack.

13. Thanks

You need to thank your friends for helping. If someone loaned you a truck, fill it with gas or leave a $20 in the glove compartment. A real friend will not take money if you hand it to them, so if you really need the $20, try to hand it to your friend instead of putting it in the glove compartment. Thank your friends that night and the next day for their help and apologize for being a dick and not listening to them and not having beer at the house and for making them work so late.

BONUS HINT

14. Take the next day off work

You will definitely want to take then next day off from work. All the stuff that you are too tired to take care of at midnight will be there for years unless you take care of it immediately. If you go to work, you are going to come home, exhausted, to unpacked boxes and no cable. If you take the next day off, you can sit around and unpack boxes while you wait for the cable guy to show up three hours late.

Comic
Jesus Emerges From the Tomb

Collection
Boots

A few years ago, I had to purchase a pair of steel-toed boots for an installation that was taking place on a construction site. My work was paying for the boots, but because I waited too long to buy them, I ended up getting a pair of steel toes in Walmart at midnight. (They are actually very comfortable and still going strong after 5 years.) When I got on the construction site, the boots were new enough that they captured the attention of one of our vendors, Rodney, who happens to be a good friend. He said that I should scuff the boots up so that they didn't look so new. I told him that reminded me of a story…

When I was 19, I went from working at a Baskin Robbins to Haning's, a roofing company in Lancaster, OH. My sister's ex-boyfriend had worked there over previous summers and said it was hard, but rewarding ($$$) work. So I applied and got a job. They said, "Wear old jeans and boots." I didn't have boots, so I went out and bought a pair. The boots glowed with newness and I thought that I would look like a punk kid if I had new boots on. I went into the yard and scuffed them up on rocks and grass to make it look like I had worn them for a while.

I showed up for work in my old jeans and "seasoned" boots. The foreman took one look at my boots and said, "Did you rub grass on your new boots?" I said, "No." He said, "It looks like you took a pair of new boots and rubbed grass on them." I said no again, but he knew.
Twenty-two years later I finish the story by telling our vendor that a pair of boots is more about what is on the inside of them and a lot less about that is on the outside of them.

He didn't believe that for a second.

Here are those boots at the end of my first summer as a roofer.

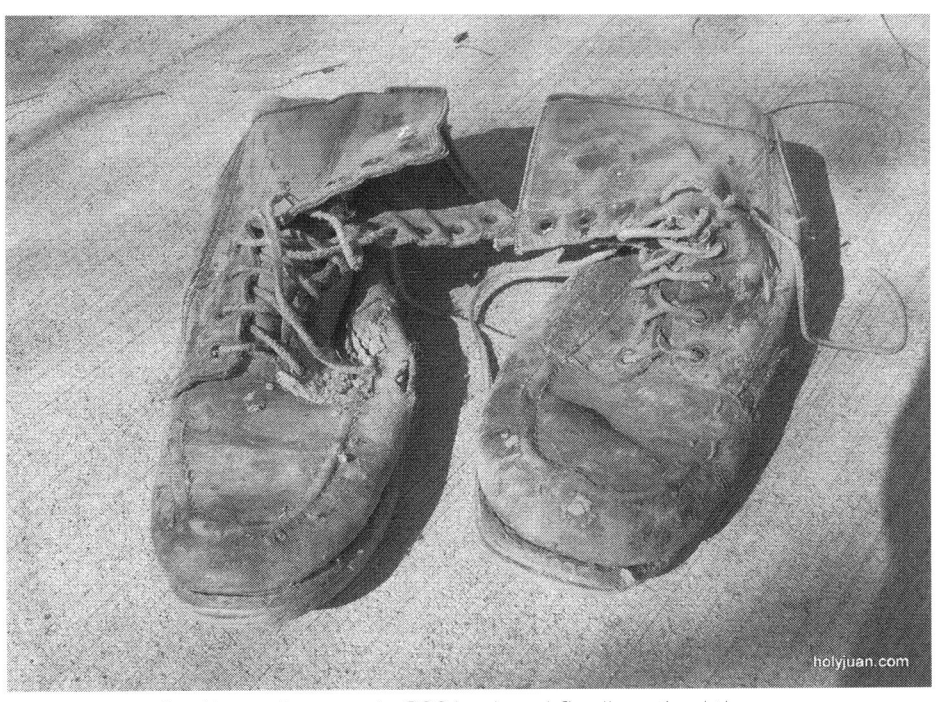

And here they are in 2006 when I finally retired them.

List
Your Relationship as Defined by Sesame Street Characters

Some people will spend a lifetime trying to figure out their relationship. Using simple correlations between Sesame Street characters and typical, screwed up relationships, I have created a way for you to understand where you are in your love sphere and how quickly that bubble will probably burst.

The Kermit and Miss Piggy
This is the most basic of all relationships. The girl knows exactly what she wants. The guy isn't so sure. Pretty soon, she convinces him through a combination of sweet talk, screaming and simple karate chops that they should be together forever.

The Grover
You have no idea why you are dating this person. They drive you nuts. They don't know what they want. They annoy the f*ck out of you. All you know is that they give good hugs and you can't help but love them.

The Cookie Monster
Desire is the foundation to any relationship. Cookie Monster desires only one thing. Men only desire one thing. Men will promise you dinner for the cookie. They will promise you faithfulness for the cookie. They will marry you for the cookie. Once you stop giving them the cookie or if the cookie starts to have less chips and more saturated fats, they may look for another cookie jar. C is for cookie, that's good enough for me.

The Snuffleupagus
The worst kind of a relationship. You tell all your friends about this great person that you've met and they don't believe you because they never actually seen them. You tell your friends to meet you out at the bar and when they show up, your date has just left. What's worse is that they begin to think you are completely crazy and when they do meet this person, they think that they are a paid escort and will never take you seriously again. You start to think that maybe your lover doesn't want anyone to know about the relationship. But your doubt is overcome by your love. You are f*cked, Bird.

The Sugapuelffuns or The Reverse Snuffleupagus
This is a relationship where you do not what your friends to know about your lover. They will see you with someone, ask about who they are and you will reply, "I don't know who you are talking about." You'll be seen together at a restaurant and later deny it. You will avoid each other at parties, but sneak out at the same

time. You lover will ask, "When will I get to meet your friends?" and you will not have a good answer. This relationship is destined not to end well.

The Bob
You are too smart and witty to realize that YOU ARE GAY! Quit wearing Maria as a beard and sing this phrase after me, "H is for Homosexual, that's good enough for me!"

The Oscar the Grouch
When given the choice between adapting to societal norms or living alone in a garbage can, you made the right decision. You are the smartest person alive. And the grumpiest because you aren't getting any.

The Elmo
Sometimes the shy type will win you over. Mainly because you can dominate them and make them do whatever you want. Going out with friends for ten nights in a row can strain a relationship. When you date an Elmo, just give them a little tickle and head out the door. If you bring home another "friend" for the evening, go inside alone and turn Elmo to face the pillows. What Elmo doesn't know can't hurt Elmo.

The Count von Count
Two words: anal retentive. If you are dating the Count, be prepared to be told how many times you've left the seat up/down and how many days it's been since you've said "I love you." Sure, the eyepiece is romantic at first, but you will soon grow weary of the cape cleaning bills, the sharp nose pokes to the eye and the fangs. The only good thing is that you will know when they are done criticizing you once the lightning bolt strikes. Ah ah ah!

The Ernie and Bert
You will probably be very happy in this bi-polar relationship, but you will also be very gay.

The Gordon and Susan
The perfect relationship. She loves him. He loves her. Sometimes they fight, but they always work it out in the end. The reason why this relationship works so well has to do with love, but has to do more with the fact that she thinks she is slightly better than him and he thinks he is slightly better than her. As long as they keep that to themselves, they will always be together.

The Linda
You act tough during the day about how being single is empowering and that no other person or disability can keep you from reaching your goals as an individual. At night you masturbate yourself to sleep and wake up more depressed than the day before when you can't hear the alarm clock go off.

The Yip Yips
No one understands your relationship. No one needs to. You go everywhere together. You both need each other to survive. You may disagree with each other at first, but you will always agree in the end. You read the same Earth book, book books. You run off the same clock. Bong! Bong! And at the end of a long day, you swallow your own head and rest peacefully until the next morning. Oh, did I mention no sex?

The Mr. Hooper
You are too old to care. You just want the stupid kids to buy something and get out. You'll die lonely, but content.

The Luis and Maria
You cannot have this relationship because it is fake. For years, many were conned into thinking that this couple were married in real life. They were not. Like Mary, mother of Jesus, Maria was knocked up by someone else and poor Luis had to take the blame. They raised the child together on the show, but we all know who the real father is. I'm looking at you, **inchworm**.

How To
How to Fabricate Your Own Bible

Making your own bible can not only be satisfying, it can guarantee your entry ticket into heaven or whatever afterlife you create! Follow these simple steps to make your own physical manifestation of your deity's (deities') words.

Rule One: Paradoxes
The only way your Bible can be successful is if it cannot be disproven. The only way to make sure this can't happen is to build a few logical dead ends. Don't immediately suggest that your god is infallible. Rookie mistake. By suggesting that your god is always right, you get people pointing at platypuses and suicide bombers and that causes doubt. You should instead say that your god is always going to test his people. And, of course, always have your god always answer questions with a question.

If all that fails, make the starting entry of your bible be the following, indisputable statement: "First!"

Rule Two: Make up rules
No bible is complete without a list of rules that cannot be broken under penalty of crappy afterlife. The wackier the rule, the more that people will believe that there is some heavenly inspiration for it:

- Thou shalt not prance
- Thou shalt not eat cheese with a fork
- Thou shalt not wear of metal the hat unless in battle for your Lord
- Eat only of the left hand
- Thou shall not recycle brown glass
- Thou shalt turn left three times after passing thy gas
- Thou shall lean backwards while showering to show thine glory of thine breasts heavenward

If you are having trouble thinking of rules, just think of the things you really like to do and forbid people from doing them.

Rule Three: Make your bible big and thick and old looking
No one believes in a book that looks like it came right off a printing press. Make your bible brownish with a slight moldy smell. Your bible should also be extremely thick. Your god's words will be much more believable if they are hand written in script. You can also make the last 2000 pages blank and tell your followers that once they are true believers that the text will become legible. Sit back and wait to hear what bullshit the true believers come up with in your god's name.

Rule Four: No chick gods
Women are way too understanding to be gods. Your god should be a raging man god. Even if your god isn't the type that would have humans be made in his image (gasp), it should still be a male-esque plate of spaghetti / creature / misty-cloudly-like entity. I would avoid giving your god a full chest of hair. Stick with flowing locks or flames.

Rule Five: Your god kicks other gods' asses
I would highly suggest including passages where your god takes out false gods in a bar fight or gun battle. Describe other gods as pansies or misguided angels that quit your god's team once they found out they couldn't make partner. Make sure that he doesn't destroy all of the false gods, just roughs them up a bit. OK, he can kill all but one of them, so that weak ass, false god can go back and tell everyone what a bad ass your god is.

Rule Six: Make an awesome afterlife
Why die and go to a cloudy place where you have to spend eternity with grandma? Instead, build an afterlife with roller coasters with no lines. Make the pure white

robes optional. Why not have Sandals create the all-inclusive afterlife with no kids? You must hint at the possibility that your followers can peer into the showers of the living to ensure they are following the list of rules.

I also highly suggest you allow your followers' pets into your heaven. You'll get a lot more followers this way. And less kids crying and hating your god.

Rule Seven: Create a lot of loopholes
    Sin is bad. Sin in the name of your god is GOOD!
    It is forbidden to kill… everyone but non-believers.
    You cannot eat cheese with a fork… unless it is the third Wednesday after the second Tuesday.

It's OK if your story has a lot of holes in it. 500 years from now, they'll just say that some of the documentation is missing and that your god is infallible and this is a test.

Comic
Jesus Reads the Bible

You would think that someone would have asked for my permission before writing this stuff.

Collection
Half Tie, Beer Leg... Two Tales of Friction

Here are two related tales that I like to call, "Half Tie" and "Beer Leg" which both hold hands with our good friend, friction. Enjoy.

Half Tie
Handsome Joe and I used to wear ties out drinking when we were in college at Ohio University. It seemed like a good way to pick up classy chicks. I had an awesome flowered tie that was obnoxious and suave. I wore it out one snowy night in Athens.

The ties didn't work and Handsome Joe and I headed home alone together. On the way, we ran into a number of students who were sliding down Jeff Hill on stolen cafeteria trays and cardboard boxes. Half-drunk kids would slide down the frozen, brick street, screaming the whole way. At the bottom, they would generously hand off their makeshift sleds, giving guys in ties a chance to take a turn.

With our borrowed stolen cafeteria trays, we ran up the stairs that paralleled the street with drunken stamina. At the top of the brick street, I took a running dive and flew down the hill. It was exhilarating.

At the bottom, I handed off the tray to another student. Handsome Joe almost took me out as he flew by. He handed off his sled and noticed that my tie was sticking half out of my jacket. Actually, it was all sticking out of my jacket, but all now was only half. The other half of it was missing.

My tie got caught under the tray as I slid down. The brick street, though nicely iced, caused a bit of friction. The tie was frayed. It was half destroyed, which means that it was all the way destroyed. I still wonder why I didn't choke to death. God bless the Double Windsor.

Beer Leg
On another beautiful snowy Athens evening, Handsome Joe, our other friend Knitter and I were stealing beer out of a friend's screened-in porch. It wasn't really stealing, because it was rightfully ours. If we had we been inside the house at the party, we would have polished the entire case of beer no problem. But since we didn't like anyone at the party, we walked out, went around back and took our beer to go.

The porch was locked, but the window was not. I crawled through the narrow, screened window, flopped on the porch floor and passed the case of beer out to

Knitter and Handsome Joe. Someone from the inside started to come outside so I dove out the window and we ran laughing through the back yards.

At Mill Street Hill, I took the case of beer from Knitter and did a running dive down the icy sidewalk on top the case of beer. It was just like a sled! I made it about half way down the hill before I ran out of ice. Knitter and Joe caught up with me laughing and we continued home with me carrying my beer sled.

Once we got back to 19 Palmer Street, I made two observations and one conclusion:
1. My right pant leg was wet.
2. About eight beers had holes in the bottom of them and they were bleeding out

Conclusion: The case of beer's cardboard armor did not stand up to my weight forcing it into the ice and then bare concrete. The cardboard was eaten through in half circles by the edges of the cans and the smiling faces were drooling beer. The case somehow retained structural integrity enough so that the beer could leak out and on to my jeans. 16 beers is not as good as 24, but always better than zero.

Friction is a bitch.

Ask HolyJuan
Is Sex for 30 Days Straight a Good Idea?

Dear HolyJuan,

I am hesitant to ask this question, mainly because I know I will get a smart ass answer and secondly because I know I will get a smart ass answer. But here it goes:

A local church here in Tampa is marketing or promoting a "30 Day of Sex" campaign where married parishioners are asked to have sex every day for 30 days and unmarried parishioners are asked to not have sex for 30 days. Somehow this is supposed to help both types of relationships.

Do you feel that this is a positive campaign or is the church just trying to get in the headlines?

Signed,

Chris

Dear Chris,

First off Chris, every single one of my "Ask HolyJuan" answers is carefully crafted to contain relevant content and appropriate language. That being said, here is your smart ass answer.

The answer to all questions church related is to ask yourself, "What Would HolyJuan Do?" Well, shit… I guess that's what you did by asking me this question in the first place. We've got the first part down!

I believe that this is just awful. When I think back to all the times I was in church as a child and when I look around in that memory, I see a lot of ugly couples. Now, throw on top of that the thought that when those two really ugly and wrinkly old people woke up that morning, the second thing they did after choking down the day's pills was to create a sweaty, wrinkle pile. A throbbing mass of liver spotted flesh, writhing in and about itself. The thought of that makes me sick.

The last time I tried something similar to this 30 day sex marathon, it was with gummy bears. My folks gave me what I thought was the greatest gift in the world: a five pound bag of gummy bears. I immediately tore into the bag and that sweet, plastic smell sent me into an eating frenzy. I ate and ate. I paused for an hour and ate again. At first I thought that I couldn't get sick of them. After two days I did, but I could not stop eating. I'd pass the bag in my room and almost gag, but somehow I'd be popping them in my mouth. I was disgusted with myself, but ate my way through it.

I finished off the bag in about four days. Three weeks later, I finally was able to take a crap and the toilet bowl was filled with Technicolor swirls and streaks. The bathroom smelled like a strip club.

Was I happy? Did over indulgence set me straight? Did I respect the gummy bears more after I stuffed my gullet with them? Did the part about the toilet make you about gag?

So where was I? The moral to the story is that if you can con your spouse into having sex with you for 30 days in a row…. great! If you can't, change religions to the one advertised in Tampa or start your own religion and force your spouse to have sex with you. If all that fails… I suggest masturbating to the "casual encounters" photos on Craig's List. At least someone is getting it.

Yours, HolyJuan

Comic
Cheaper Alternative for Gasoline

List
Ten Things Parents Will Never Admit

As it turns out, parents do dumb, stupid and idiotic things and you'd never know because no one talks about it. Here are a few of those things that they will never admit to doing. I am an extremely good parent and deny any such activities. Deny, deny, deny.

1. Spanking
This is the biggie that very few parents fess up to, but of which some are guilty at various levels. Physical punishment really does not work in the long run. But when your kid keeps pushing your buttons and the button on top your buttons, you just want to smack them upside the head. Of course, I know you don't.

2. Laugh at their suffering
For the eighth time you told little Billy to not run through the kitchen with his socks. The ninth time he slips and falls and hits his little head. Scooping him up, you rub the knot on the back of his head, quietly snickering to yourself, "I told you so..."

3. Lie
I know we lie to our children for their own good. Santa. The tooth fairy. Sex. God. But sometimes we lie just because we f*cked up and cannot let them know that we are mortal. Lies like, "I didn't say that," when you did, or "We'll get a toy next time," when you won't. Be careful. Those little bastards have a rock solid memory and will call you out. If they do, see #1.

4. Forget to buckle them in their car seat
When precious is fighting from getting in the car seat and your cell phone rings you might forget to strap your kid in. It happens. You get to where you are going and when you go to unfasten the kid, they are already unbuckled. That's when you pretend to unbuckle them so that they don't know the difference and don't say to the other parent that you didn't buckle them in last time. That will get you all sorts of "unfit parent" BS from the other spouse when you know full well they have forgotten too.

5. Eat the last of the child's fun food
I have had the last fruit rollup about thirty times.

6. Make frozen pancakes when there's mix in the cupboard and eggs in the refrigerator.

This one covers a lot of bases. Basically it is taking a short-cut when you should actually be doing "the right thing." This includes letting your kid watch TV when you should be interacting with them, calling grandma instead of going to visit and allowing your kid have a TV in their room (the greatest of all parental sins. You know who you are.)

7. Forget about a child

This one can end in tragedy, but this is a light hearted piece so we will keep it on the up and up. Most the time you forget, it ends up with you leaving for work, going back in to grab your coffee and seeing junior sitting quietly on the couch waiting for you to take him to school. Oops! Or getting home from work and having your spouse ask you if you picked up junior from practice. Oops! Most parents have done it, but they'll never tell.

8. Cuss in front of the kids

If you get cut off in traffic, you will drop an f-bomb. If you hit your hand with a hammer, you will say "shit." If you burn your hand on the stove, you're guaranteed a resounding "mother f*ck." When little Sarah comes home from school with a note saying she said "F*ck shit mother f*ck," you will blame the neighbor kid. It worked in "A Christmas Story" and it works for you... with this one, you are really lying to yourself, but you know the truth.

9. Listen to inappropriate music with the kids around

I will listen to Howard Stern on satellite radio until someone cusses or they start talking about VA-GI-NAS. This means I get to listen for about fifteen seconds. Some parents are OK with listening to graphic rap or crappy pop in front of their kids. I like hearing my son going around singing, "Hey, hey, you, you, I don't like your girlfriend," or "Go Shorty, it's your burfday. We gonna drink Bacardi like it's mah burfday." I have to pretend like he heard it at the neighbor kid's birthday party. (Which he did. (Really.))

10. Let your kid see you naked

Your kid will see you naked. Hopefully not during your fifteen seconds of awkward lovemaking. The question is at what age do you cut them off without making it look like you are trying to hide your bits and pieces? The answer is that healthy, good looking people can be naked all the time around their kids. It gives the children an excellent example to live up to. If you are an ugly mess, cover your shame as no kid needs to see that. But either way, don't let other people know you are naked around your kid. That's just sick.

Collection
My First Beer Bong

Have you ever bonged a beer? The beer bong is a wonderful invention. If you dislike the taste of beer and also don't like to waste your time chit chatting at parties waiting for the buzz to kick in, then fear no more! There was a time in my life where I was unfamiliar with that MacGyveresqe contraption which employs a funnel, three feet (or sometimes thirty) of tubing and a hose clamp. It's actually possible to buy a manufactured beer bong off the shelf in towns that you only go to once for Spring Break. Just avoid the used ones. The best beer bongs are acquired via spare parts by sifting through the garage and under the kitchen sink.

Before we knew of beer bongs, Russ and I went on a road trip with the Widener twins to Bowling Green State University. We met up with our buddy Brett and went to a party at an apartment. While we were all enjoying a few Keystone Light pounders, the host pulled out what I soon found out was a beer bong. He proceeded to fill the funnel end with beer while another partygoer deftly held the tube pinched closed at the other end. The host held the funnel up, the guy went down on one knew, tube went into his mouth and chug chug chug... it was gone! Beer one second, no beer in three seconds. Amazing! How does that work? I can imagine Julius Sumner Miller explaining the physics behind the beer bong:

"I point out that we have a funnel. In addition, there is a plastic tubing of length being one meter. Are you not agreed that these two are connected? Yes. Now supposing we take this 12 ounce cylindrical container of beer. Where is the beer? Where? Yes, here it is. And pour this beer in the funnel. Oh mercy, it poured out on the floor of the lab. Goddamn it Mr. Anderson! You were supposed to bend the length of tubing! Hellfire!" (I think we were all waiting for Julius Sumner Miller to snap. I loved the guy.)

A few other people used the beer bong and I was given the opportunity to try it. Pinch, fill, mouth, release... chug, squirt, choke, beer in nose, gag, chug... It was a lot harder than it looked. This was going to take some practice.

In the background, a soft voice seemed to rise up. "I'd like to try that, please." It was Russ (I think he was raising his hand.) "Sure!"

Pinch, fill, mouth, release... s'gunk. It was gone. I mean, he just downed the thing in a quarter second on his first try. The host was impressed. The crowd roared! Russ was a GOD! He shrugged his shoulders and explained, "I just opened my throat and it went down." Russ found his purpose in life.

We drank a lot. Russ continued to impress the locals with his bonging prowess. I continued to get beer all over me.

The next day we drove back to Lancaster. We were giddy with excitement about sharing our newly found technology with everyone in Lancaster. It would make slow beer drinking obsolete. We both had to work that night at the Baskin Robbins. An hour before work, we went into an auto parts store and gathered all the necessary components. We would be the first people in Lancaster to own a bong. The checkout guys said, "You all gonna make a beer bong?"
"You know what a beer bong is?"
"Hell, I thought everyone knew what a beer bong was. That'll be $5.78."

OK, so we were pretty stupid. Turns out the beer bong had been around a while and we just weren't invited to the right parties. Still, we had a bong and we were going to practice.

At work, we built the beer bong. We wanted to practice so we tried bonging water, but it was too plain. We tried bonging coke, but the carbonation almost took Russ out. We then got the bright idea to bong iced coffee. It had some flavor and no one was going to explode from carbonation buildup.

Two pots of coffee later...

Russ and I were vibrating around the store. I could almost scoop the ice cream through sheer willpower. Russ levitated about three feet off the ground in the corner. We'd pee in shifts and speak to each other only through our thoughts.

As we were closing for the night, our buddy Greg arrived. It seemed that a bunch of punk ass kids ganged up on him in the local Kroger's parking lot. He was able to drive off and was looking for some reinforcements. We were primed to kick some ass. We all jumped into Greg's car and went back to the Kroger's, flexing and shouting the whole way.

Sadly for this story, nothing happened. The kids were gone. We ran around in circles for a few minutes and then got breakfast at the Family Restaurant. I remember coming down pretty hard. Not being able to sleep. Night sweats. 24 trips to the bathroom.

The last time I saw that bong was years later at a friend's apartment. It had tape patching it up and smeared black marker on the funnel. It had a funk that couldn't be washed out. I think it was cursed it when, while one person was bonging a beer, someone poured a wine cooler in with the beer. The guy using it at the time puked right back in and up through the bong.

The best $5.78 we ever spent.

List/How To
Seven Things You Can Do to Help Your Relationship

Here are seven tips to help keep your relationship happy and healthy.

Write it down
If you have something to say, say it on paper. Write down your feelings and issues. Sort them out, get rid of the anger and construct a valid statement. Then sit them down at the kitchen table and say it. DO NOT GIVE YOUR SIGNIFICANT OTHER A NOTE – unless you are dumping them, then you can leave a note.

Don't internet cheat
If you are having an affair online, you are in a very, very, deep, darkish dark grey area. Internet relationships are just practice for cheating in real life. Though I think the only place that men and women can actually be friends is on the internet, if you start thinking that a relationship via the internet is harmless, you are mistaken. Some internet forums are a great place to seek advice and to anonymously get issues off your chest. But when you start innocently flirting and it progresses, your real relationship will suffer. It will suffer even more when your spouse uses your AIM logs and e-mails in court.

Do scheduled stuff together
I hate to say this, but "date night" works. When my buddies say they can't go out drinking because they have date night, I can't help but roll my eyes and start throwing out the manly insults. Of course, when it's my date night and my buddies call and start to chide me, I tell them they are insensitive and do not understand how a good relationship works.

Sex is also great on a schedule. You and your spouse should work out one day a week that you decide to have sex. Of course, Miss Sally will get into bed and I will say, "It's Have Sex Tuesday!" And Miss Sally will say, "But wasn't last night Have Sex Monday?" That's when I reach under the bed and pull out the calendar marked "Tuesday" that has all the Tuesdays marked with a red circle. Just don't let your significant other look under the bed and see the other six calendars.

Say it on a daily basis
"You are pretty."
"I like that shirt on you."
"You look great."
"I miss you."
"Have a good day."
"You smell great."
"That was a nice dinner."
"Kiss me."
"I love you."

Get away. But not too far away
I am a big fan of guys' night out. I am also a fan of wife night out. It's good for both individuals in the relationship to have other friends and other hobbies that can get them away for a few hours. Just make sure that you balance that time with your own time together. Miss Sally bought me an anniversary card that read, "My husband and I go out two nights a week. He goes out on Thursdays and I go out on Saturdays." Sadly, I need to take my own advice on this one.

If you do get involved in a hobby, ensure that it does not take up all your time or involve Team Fortress 2 or World of Warcraft. Those are relationship killers.

Exercise
This one is the hardest of all for me, but it's probably the smartest of all the suggestions listed here. Exercise keeps you healthy. Makes you better in the sack. Keeps off the pounds. Make you look good. Keeps you alive for longer so that you can spend more time with the ones you love. It makes you feel good.

I, of course, do not exercise because I fear that if I get any better looking, it will actually threaten my marriage with all the chicks noticing me. For the sanctity of my marriage, I'll hold off from working out. I will make this sacrifice for love.

Massage
I can guarantee that if you make time for massage, you will get laid. If you don't know how to massage, buy a book. It is a very intimate and a relationship building opportunity. And did I mention you can guarantee sex? Because you will definitely get some action. And if the guys are not into getting a massage, I would highly suggest the B for B or Rub and Tug. That's where the man gives the woman a back rub and the woman gives the guy a back rub except that you replace the phrase "woman gives a backrub" with "woman gives a blowjob."

Comic
Nuns Know

Collection
0 - 1 - 3 - 1 - 0 Theory

The 0, 1, 3, 1, 0 Theory fits for most guys. It's a chart that traces the lifecycle of a guy's dating gradient by counting the number of girls in his life. If you are a dude, you are somewhere on this chart. Where you are and how long you stay there makes you a stud or whatever the opposite of a stud is.

0 Girls– This is where all guys start out and where many find themselves most of the time. No girls in their life. None interested. No secret admirers. No play. Zip.

1 Girl- Somehow, a guy finds a girl and for some unknown reason, she likes him. They begin to hang out. Life is good. For some guys (Amish) this is where the buggy stops. They meet one girl and that's it for the rest of their life. For the rest of us, read on.

3 Girls – It is my belief that some girls cannot like a guy because they like him. These girls like a guy because other girls like him. When some dude gets a girl, other girls notice immediately and start to move in on him. The #1 girl could be from another school, but the hopeful #2 and #3 can smell it on the dude that he's got someone who likes him. The guys that can spend their life at this stage, balancing more than one woman in their life impress me. Three girls can actually be 4 or 5, as long as the guy can juggle them and they allow themselves to be juggled. For the rest of us, this "3 girls" stage is a very short lived one.

1 Girl – The boy commits and he is back down to one girl in his life. For some reason, guys, who are built to have sex with as many women as possible, want to whittle it down to just one girl. Maybe it's because guys get weary of all the sex. Or maybe it's because guys get tired of listening about how #1, #2 and #3's day went and how was yours and let's stay in tonight and watch Netflix. Or it's because of Love. I don't know. All I know is the boy texts the #2 and #3 girls and tell them that he's made a difficult choice and if it is OK to have sex one last time and they never respond again.

0 Girls – She dumps his ass. Time for him to listen to Disintegration by The Cure in his bedroom for a few nights straight or get really drunk and puke in a potted flower at the nudie bar. He needs to get over it because he is going to be at this stage for a while. #2 girl and #3 girl are not returning his texts and rejecting his calls. Girls can smell desperation and they don't like it. (On the flip side, guys can smell desperation and they like to have sex with it.)

So that's it. The cycle begins again. 0-1-3-1-0. There are variations: the 0-1-2-1-0. The 0-1-0. My personal old favorite is the Hefner: 0-1-945.

Me? I'm at the second 1. I've been trying to talk the wife into the 0-1-3-1-2-1-2-1-2-1, but she's not interested.

The girl chart is simple. A girl can be at both 0 and 9 at the same time. She can be at 1 at breakfast and 4 by brunch. For some reason, millions of dollars are spent each year with girls trying to find the right 1. Little do they know their own power. Luckily, no chicks read Holyjuan.com and our secret is safe guys.

List
Parental Myths That No Parent Will Tell You About

Here are a few items that every parent, pre-parent or misguided parent should know. Sorry Mom and Dad.

Parents love their children equally
Bottom line, one kid is always going to be better, and thus liked more, than the others for some unknown, visceral reason. Either because he or she was the first or have more personality or they are smarter than the others. Parents also seem to like the child that physically resembles them the most. I'm not saying there is a whole lot of difference in the amount of love, but deep in the back of their minds, parents already have their "Sophie's Choice" choice made up. If you are an only child, congrats. If you are adopted and there are natural brothers and sisters, you are screwed.

Parents check in to see how their child is sleeping
Parents "check in" on their kids every so often during nap or night time. As an outsider, you may think that it is simply to see if the child is awake. In actuality, it is to see if the kid is dead or not breathing. The relief gained from having a not-dead child is priceless.

Having two kids is twice as hard as having one kid
Sadly that's wrong. Here is the math:
- Having one child is like having one child
- Having two children is like having four children
- Having three kids is like having five kids
- Having four kids is like having two kids.

When you have one kid, as a parental team, have shared the responsibility of taking care of one kid. Once you have two, that whole little unwritten sharing contract is out the door. You now must put out four times the effort to manage the two kids. Once you have three kids, the ratio starts to go down. Four kids might as well be none because you can split them into two teams and pit them against each other. If you have five kids, obviously the other wives can help to take care of all the little darlings.

Scientific studies say that sugar actually does *not* make your child hyper
Wrong. Sugar does make your kid hyper and I don't care what scientific studies say as I have seen the effects. Not only does it make them hyper during and after consumption, it makes them pre-hyper. If kids know about the existence of candy within a five mile radius, which they do, they will desire it. Because kids only know

how to eat and how to crap, that candy will fill 90% of their reality. And their reality will be jumping up and down and screaming. They want it and that's it. Once you give it to them, they want more. If you deny them, they will kid bitch and a kid bitching sucks.

My child is advanced
Every parent believes that her kid is somehow smarter than other kids and she will share this information with you often and repeatedly. Wrong. Your child is just as not-smart as the rest. He or she may be advanced in some area, but that's the only area the parent will focus. Kids are only as smart as you let them be. I suggest a daily dose of brow beatings to drop of heavy load of self-doubt on your kid. Self-doubters work harder and make more money so they can take care of you later in life. Unless your little Einsteins are reading and writing at age three, go sit down. If they are reading and writing at age three, my kid with low self-esteem is going to beat them up.

Having kids ruins your sex life
Ok, you've got me on this one.

Comic
What Are You Thinking About Honey?

How To
How to Know When a Relationship is Over

Your relationship has been dragging and you know that it might soon be over. You throw everything you have into keeping it together, but something just isn't right. Here are a few ways to know when a relationship is done for:

1. They aren't at home anymore
If you wake up and your lover is not there, it might be because they got up early to go to work and get the McGruder project back on track. When they do not come home that night, they might be working late and forgot to call. When you check and see that all of his/her clothes are gone, maybe it is because he/she went on a business trip and neglected to remind you. When your significant other doesn't come back from that business trip for over a month, you can be sure that he/she has left you.

2. Wife puts her maiden name on Facebook
Nothing says "game over" like your wife putting her maiden name up on Facebook. The deal is that most the people you and she interact with know your wife by her married name. When she puts her maiden name up on Facebook, she's basically advertising to all the guys she knew in high school and college that she's still out there and available if things don't work out with you.

3. You wake up dead
There is a split second between deep sleep and death when you realize that some shit has gone down. Waking up with a gunshot wound is a sure sign that things just aren't working out. Try not to bleed on the carpet; your spouse has got to resell this home once you have passed on.

4. You are not having sex, but your spouse is
When your spouse rolls in drunk at 3:30am and immediately jumps into the shower, you might accept the excuse that they were sweaty from jogging. At 3:30am. Since they have taken a shower, you ask if they want to have sex and they say, "No, I've had enough tonight," you can pretty much assume that it's over.

5. Your shit is in the driveway
If you can't pull into the driveway because your clothes, books and favorite furniture is blocking the drive way, it could be because a reality show appeared and is filming in your house on closet reorganization. Once you notice your better half throwing it from the second story window, you'd better call your friend who owns a truck to help you cart your crap off.

6. Spouse has virtual wedding with someone else on-line
So your partner is involved in on-line games. Great! They have a hobby. When they start making life decisions based on the religious beliefs of a shaman, it's awesome that they are expanding their religious horizons. When you find them leaving for the airport to fly to Reno to meet Gruflchette for a nude ceremony under the full moon, you can pretty much delete the relationship.

7. Twilight
If your spouse is reading Twilight, you are obviously not giving them enough romance or excitement. You think Tolkien was getting laid? That man only had sex if he was writing about wood nymphs and elves getting it on. If your loved one doesn't have a bookmark because they can tear through a whole 1200 pages of Harry Potter, your relationship is finished.

8. Volunteer for the military
Remember how you were planning for that trip into wine country? Remember? And the day you were leaving, your partner said that they just had to run down to the recruiter's office for just a minute. And then you sat there with the picnic basket for a few hours wondering whether you were going to go with the pinot noir or the merlot. Three weeks later someone comes to your door asking for donations for gift packages to send to your partner who is bravely serving overseas. You are done.

9. Scream someone else's name during sex
... and you hear it as you walk in the house from work. You're done.

10. You are reading this
If you are reading this final paragraph, you must have some inclination that things are going to shit. Most people would have quit reading at #2 or at best #3. But no, you kept delving, searching for some explanation why your lover is playing WOW naked with a Twilight book on tape playing in the background. It's over Johnny. It's over.

Comic
Picasso and Pictionary

Picasso's team never won at Pictionary.

holyjuan.com

Ask HolyJuan
Flight Risk Apartment Mate Advice

Dear HolyJuan,
I'm not sure if you know much about renting and deposits, but here is my problem: I have been a good tenant, but my apartment mate has not. Due to some problems that are definitely his fault, he was unable to pay his half of the rent the last two months.

I've noticed that he has been slowly been removing his stuff from the apartment. He says that he is just cleaning up, but his computer is gone and so are his school books and I think he is going to break the lease.

Is there anything I can do to get him to pay his rent? Should I be afraid of him moving out overnight? I do not care if he is not friends with me after this because I think he's been peeing on the carpet. I also want my half of the deposit back.

Signed,

Room for rent in Ohio

Dear Room,
You are screwed. This guy is either moving out slowly or he's selling his crap for crack and sooner or later crack people will steal your shit or kill you. You'll never see the deposit and you'll be lucky if your credit isn't ruined from this asshole bailing on you.

There is only one thing to do: pre-revenge.

Step 1: Eat asparagus, wait thirty minutes, pee on his mattress and flip it over. This is just in case the rest of the steps do not work and at least you'll feel like you got partial retribution.

Step 2: Buy some cheap lamps and a few False Aralia plants. Set them up in that basement or closet that is not in your room. These plants look EXACTLY like marijuana plants.

Step 3: Call the landlord and tell him/her that you are being called back into the military because of some stopgap measure and that not letting you out of your lease is not only illegal, it's Un-American, god damnit. When he sheepishly asks for proof, download any military document you can get your hands on, use Photoshop to smudge it and fax it to him eight or nine times in a row. Tell him the fax machine at Fort Bragg is really shitty. He'll believe you. He has to!

Step 4: Move out quickly. Don't get your friends involved in the move. Use local laborers at the Home Depot or call LaborReady. Get 15 or so guys and it will take less than ten minutes.

Step 5: Put a string of black cat fireworks in a back room of the apartment with a fuse that is long enough to run out a window.

Step 6: When your apartment mate comes home, call the cops. Say you are a temp worker for LaborReady and that you saw some weed plants in a basement or closet at the apartment you moved some guy out of today.

Step 7: When the cops show up, light the fuse.

Step 8: Your apartment mate will be killed by the cops who think they are being fired on.

Step 9: Move back in and tell your landlord that your platoon received new orders.

Step 10: You will get A's for the semester because of the death of your apartment mate.

Step 11: Put a ROOMMATE NEEDED ad on Craigslist. Put it in the Casual Encounters section just for fun. You've earned it.

Hope this helps!

HolyJuan

List
Grocery Store Stereotypist

I am a grocery store stereotypist. When I am heading for the check out line, I look for a few clues that get me though the line quicker. Sometimes I make assumptions. Usually I am right and in the parking lot while you are still counting your change at the self checkout line.

1. The longest line isn't always the longest
Just because a line is further back than the rest does not essentially mean it will take the longest to get through. Check for families that are going through together. If there are four people and only one cart, chances are it will take them less time to get through than two carts taking up the same about of space.

2. Look out for split orders
When you saunter up to the line, be on the lookout for one person (usually a young woman with a baby) separating her purchases into two piles. This usually means she will be paying for part of the order with WIC or food stamps. This takes a good bit of time and a manager and explaining to the customer as to why Jell-o is not one of the approved foods.

3. Look at the nametag
If the cashier has a nametag that has a whole lot of stickers and ribbons and flair, hit their line. They have been at the store for years and know all the fruit/vegetables codes by heart including tomatillos and plantains.

4. Avoid the tobacco line
Many stores have a dedicated tobacco line. This is the only line with cigarettes. Unless the cashier is on the ball, it will take them five minutes to find the Lucky Strike Filter Soft Pack Buy Two Get One Free. You also have to worry about other cashiers coming over to pick up smokes for the people in their line that were trying to avoid standing in the Smoking Line in the first place. Smokers are also too damn chatty with the cashier. Shut up all ready.

5. Coupon people save money, not time
If you see coupons… avoid. The coupon people usually have an 85% fail rate at which one of their coupons is wrong or expired. They'll whip out their coupon sorting system and try to find the right one. Coupon people also usually pay by check, just to piss me off.

6. Checkbookers
There is no way to tell if someone is going to pay by check. I have done studies. I have read books. I have watched endless hours of security camera tapes only to come up empty handed. I once was 100% sure that the kid in front of me was going to pay with cash/credit card because he showed the sure signs of not being a checkbooker:
a) he was a dude
b) he was buying beer
c) he had no apparent checkbook

What he did have was a single, folded up check in his pocket. Luckily he was buying beer so he had his ID available. If you know of some way to tell, please let me know.

7. Self-checkout isn't always quicker
Just because you have two items doesn't mean you should definitely use the self-checkout. If there is even one person waiting to use the self-checkout, scan the cashier lines. The self-checkout always seems to have hiccups when they are full. Just last week I bypassed the self-checkout with two people waiting on the four people checking out. As I left the store, one of the two people were still standing in line to use the self-checkout.

8. Avoid old people
Sadly, old people suck at going through lines. They like to chit chat. They ask questions. They want dented boxes replaced. They like to pay with check. They don't know how to use the card scanner. They like paper instead of plastic. They forgot an item and need the bagger to be a good boy and run and get some graham crackers no the ones in the blue box, that's a dearie.

9. Dodge vegans
Vegans are complicated in lines. They tend to buy the organic vegetables which causes a mix up when no one knows the product code. They buy weird packaged which causes a fuss when no one knows when the hell the tempeh expiration date is. They bring their own bags, which is great for the environment, but screws up the bagger. They usually pay in cash, which would normally be fine except that most cashiers have never seen the stuff before. I assume the line at Whole Foods never moves.

10. You can't avoid receipt checkers
Just like with the Checkbookers, it's hard to know you are in line with a Receipt Checker until they start checking the receipt. You can notice them watching the screen as their groceries are being scanned. When the final price is stated by the cashier, you can almost feel the air being sucked into their lungs so that they can exclaim, "Oh my!" They'll pay the total, but damnit if they don't stand there, blocking your advance, going line by line through the receipt, looking for an error. And they'll question the cashier as if they keep a database of prices in their head. The manager is called in and will hopefully pull the miser off to the side to examine the receipt in detail so that you can continue with your purchases and wait until the very end to pull out your coupons and checkbook and ask for smokes.

Comic
Jesus In a Water Balloon Fight

Collection
The Container and The Contents

A group of my friends took a Spring Break trip to Myrtle Beach two years before we turned 21. That was the awkward time of wanting to acquire alcohol right before being legally able to buy it. I had tasted the devil's sweat and couldn't wait to do it again without worrying about getting busted. When on our home turf, there were always older friends to buy beer or bars that friend's dad owned. On the road and without fake IDs, it was a little tougher. That's why we decided to take our own. Not in bottles, cans or in wine skins, but in a five gallon, insulated coffee dispenser in the form of Hairy Buffalo.

There are two parts of this story: The Container and The Contents.

The Container
Eric went to school at Miami of Ohio's Western campus or as it's known to those who really care, The School of Interdisciplinary Studies/Western College Program at Miami University in Oxford, Ohio. We knew it as the hippy side of Miami U. It's a very liberal college where everyone seemed to have long hair (back when it wasn't fashionable) and hairy armpits (which is now fashionable.) Notwithstanding my mocking, it was a wonderful school and Eric loved it.

During Eric's tenure at Western, Folgers Coffee had a marketing campaign aimed at getting college kids addicted to coffee again. (This was back when Starbucks only had 125 stores. They were all within three blocks of each other, but you get my drift.) To get the kids' addiction rolling, they strategically placed 5 gallon, insulated, coffee dispensers all around the Miami and Western campuses. In the mornings, a truck would drive around with full containers. A dude would climb out of the truck, unchain the hopefully empty 5 gallon container, replace it with a full container, refill the cups and toss the empty containers and trash back in the truck. It would take the guy about ninety seconds to complete the transaction.

You may not know this, but Eric has the unique ability to borrow a 5 gallon, insulated, coffee dispenser off the back of a truck in about thirty seconds. Though it was his plan to grab an empty one, the one he borrowed was full of hot coffee. For you that are unfamiliar, five gallons of hot coffee weighs about 41.8 lbs. With the container at a slim 16 pounds, he was lugging a total hot load of 57.8 lbs. The container was tall and thin with handles at the top. One would have to lug the container with arms hanging down and legs spread apart in a sort of half crab walk.

Eighty seconds into his delivery, the coffee dude turned around to see a long haired asshole, half crab walking across the green carrying off one of his containers of coffee. Eric had a fifty second lead and all the guy could do was yell and take a few worthless steps in Eric's direction.

I'm sure this container, God knows where it is today, could tell a number of stories of the original coffee that was drank from it and the dozens of other liquids that filled it during it's time in Eric's dorm room, then law school and perhaps all the way to Chicago. Since the container is not here, I will tell the one story that I know.

The Contents
I think the whole reason we decided to take Hairy Buffalo was based on the fear of getting busted for speeding on the way down to Myrtle Beach and having the cops search our car and take away any bottles of liquor. Somehow, a huge five gallon container of red liquor fortified punch would slip by the eye of Deputy Dawg in his search for contraband.

We were divided up into two groups: those finding the required alcohol and those buying the fruit and mixers. I can't remember what group I was in. What I do remember is that Russ was in the latter group and arrived at Eric's house with rhubarb. Rhubarb? What the f*ck is rhubarb? Rhubarb is basically a weed that you find next to okra in the Natural Foods section of the supermarket. You see, Russ had been eating Rhubarb for years in his mom's cherry-rhubarb pie. As a pie, it was like tasty celery swimming with cherries and a shit ton of sugar in a crust. Why wouldn't it taste good in a hairy buff? For one thing, you have to drown rhubarb in sugar to make it palatable. It's also a good idea to bake it as well. Russ wouldn't have any of that and chopped it up along with the watermelon and strawberries.

The dudes who were in charge of alcohol did well and came back with various bottles of alcohol as well as sugary liquors like bright red DeKuypers. It was a fine collection of alcohol to mix with the juices and the fruit and the f*cking rhubarb, which I'm sure is a vegetable.

So we placed the 5 gallon container in the middle of Eric's mom's priceless, hand-woven Turkish carpet and began to pour the bottles of liquor in it. We had dumped about four bottles in when someone noticed that the container was not filling up. In fact, it was getting lower. That statement made everyone shut up just long enough for us to hear the noise of liquid pouring out of the spout on to a priceless, hand-woven Turkish carpet. We had cleaned and rinsed the container out and in doing so, the convenient spigot at the bottom of the container was open and the liquor was pouring out and on to the thirsty carpet.

This was a problem for two reasons: First, almost a third of the alcohol was not going to be leaving Ohio. Second, we just figured out how to turn priceless rug into a less-price rug. Eric was a little pissed off, but shit, it was his container. He should have checked the integrity of the tap before handing it over.

We closed the tap and pulled the container away from the spillage area. There was a red stain about one foot in diameter. Towels were brought in and we scrubbed and cleaned as best we could. I'm unsure if Zud is the best stain remover for Turkish carpets, but that's what we found under the kitchen sink.

We cleaned the top as best we could and then rolled back the carpet to see what had happened to the underside. The padding under the carpet was unlike anything I had ever seen. It was like a natural mesh of unwoven reeds or weeds or jute. Whatever it was, it was soaked in liquor. The natural material had taken a liking to the liquor and wasn't about to let go of the red coloration. We soaked up what we could and laid the carpet back down.

There was still a red stain on the carpet at the point of impact. It was about the size of the bottom of a vacuum cleaner. As luck would have it, Eric had a vacuum cleaner and we placed it directly over the stain. No one would ever suspect a thing. At least until we were out of state. Three hours later we were out of state with a 5 gallon, insulated coffee container that was not full enough of hairy buffalo. The rhubarb absorbed the red liquid along it's veins and looked like diseased flesh and tasted almost as bad. I think Russ ate them all.

I found a photo of the dudes from the Spring Break trip.

From left to right: Eric, Brett, Russ, Greg and Tony. Kit is smack dab in the middle. (I'm taking the photo. I might have been wearing a t-shirt that said "Nothing phases a ceramic engineer.")

Collection
An Oil Cap

On that same trip to Myrtle Beach, South Carolina, Kit, Russ and I drove down in Kit's car while Greg, Tony and Brett drove in Greg's truck. Eric kept switching cars at the service stations to avoid paying for gas.

Not more than an hour outside of Cincinnati, Greg's truck pulled up from behind us and made hand gestures to suggest that they were not very happy. A few seconds later, Kit's oil light came on. We all did the coincidence math and pulled over at the next exit. Greg's windshield was covered in a thin film of oil. They thought we were spraying liquid or oil out a window at them. One smell from Kit's engine and we could tell it was leaking oil a few drips at a time. We (and by we, I mean Kit) bought a case of motor oil at highway robbery prices (now I know were the term "highway robbery" comes from) and continued to head south-east.

For the rest of the trip, we would pull over every 50 miles or so and top off the oil with a quart. Not the most environmental thing to do, but the environment didn't exist back in the late 80's. When my turn came, I jumped out with a can of oil, checked the dip stick, removed the cap, added most the quart, checked the dip stick for my perfection and shut the hood.

(You may see where this is going.)

In less than five miles, the oil light was back on and there were CLOUDS of smoke coming from under the hood. Kit pulled over, expecting that the little hole had grown into something bigger. He opened the hood and there was oil everywhere except on the oil cap because there was no oil cap. The oil cap was probably four miles back in the road. Or perhaps in some odd twist of fate, it ended up with my gasoline cap, together in some auto parts love story. But enough of that, let's get to the part where Kit was mad.

Kit was mad. He didn't show it very well, but you could tell he was pissed because he didn't say much and there was the gritting of teeth and clenching of fists. I kept suggesting that we could stick a shirt in the hole. We started thinking about what raw materials we had that we could carve or construct into a make-shift oil cap.

And then Russ suggested something that was both crazy and genius: let's try the gas cap on it. Closer inspection revealed that Kit's gas cap was not the screw in variety but rather the round with two tabs sticking out either side variety. Russ took the gas cap and made the rest of the trip possible because it fit, snugly, right in the oil cap hole. It was both a gas cap and an oil cap.

On the way back from that God awful vacation, a miracle happened. Kit took the car in to a shop to get his oil leak checked out. It was a vacation town shop and we were a bunch of dudes from Ohio with an oil leak. They mechanic could have really screwed Kit over, but instead he said that if we kept topping off the oil, the car would make it back to Ohio where he could get it fixed for a lot cheaper.

And he also gave us a pretty good deal on the case of oil to get us back to Ohio. (And by us, I mean Kit.)

List
The Secret Meaning of Road Signs

You've seen these road/traffic signs, but do you know what they really mean?

Short Cut
Many of us know this as "No Through Trucks," but it really means "This is a short-cut to somewhere else." Truckers know the quickest routes from point A to point B and neighborhoods get mad when trucks short-cut through their streets. The neighbors will clamor for the city to erect signs that politely ask the trucks not to come through, but at the same time give everyone else a clear marking for a short-cut. Thanks, suckers!

Crash Into Me
This is a directional warning sign. It tells you that there is imminent danger on one side of the sign and safety on the other. But which side is which? The safe side is the one where the black and yellow stripes point down. (In this case, the safe side is the left side. I think.) By the time you do the visual math in your head it is going to be too late. It's best to play it safe and ram you car straight into the sign. Sure, your car is totaled, but it beats falling off a cliff. There is also no guarantee that the road worker dude installed the sign correctly. Until they start putting arrows on these signs, play it safe and ram it.

Snakes Following Your Car
This one is obvious, but I had to include it.

Left Hand Turn with Attitude
A U-turn is just an extended left hand turn. If you take the same precautions with a U-turn as a left hand turn, plus the additional lookout for traffic turning into you, U-turns should not be outlawed. In Ohio they are illegal, but only when you get caught. I would suggest that you explain to the officer pulling you over that you were making a left hand turn and got carried away. Ohio cops are pretty jovial.

Deer Jumping Over Your Car
My problem with this sign is that it fools you into thinking that the deer is jumping over the road and harmlessly over your car. I can see why any average driver would think that with the scale of this sign.

Let's take the car from the "Snakes Following Your Car" sign and put it on the "Deer Jumping Over Your Car" sign.

See! Right over the top. They need to make the sign with the deer standing in the middle of the road, staring dumbly straight at you, which is exactly what you see right before you hit a deer.

Please, Please, Please Go This Slow
If you see a yellow speed limit sign, it is just a speed suggestion. (It's difficult to tell from this image that this sign is yellow with black lettering. Once I am rich, I'll be able to afford to print in color.) This sign is hoping that you go this slow when legally, you can go the posted speed limit. Some worry wart at the Division of Transportation will sleep soundly tonight, knowing that his road will be suggestively safer due to his request that you please go slower. I suggest going the posted speed limit and as you lose control of your car, crash in to the little yellow sign.

Please Let Me In (or) Get Out of My Way!
Yield is the only sign that has two completely different meanings depending on what angle you are looking at it from. If I am the one yielding, it means that I need to speed up to engage the traffic and slip into the stream of cars that will kindly allow me to merge into the happy community of commuters.
On the other hand, if you are yielding to me, this sign means that you need to come to a complete stop to gain entry into MY lane. You are MY bitch. Get behind me. Don't try to speed up and sneak in because I can LEGALLY run you off the road. This sign also summarizes what politics are like between the party in power and the minority party.

Don't Be Polite

This looks like a normal four-way stop sign. It is actually the lurking place of people who think they are being nice. If you are the first one at a four-way stop sign, you get to go through the intersection first. If two people show up at the exact same time, the person to the right of you goes first (and you might be the person on the right so get moving.) If four people show up at the same time, it's every man for himself. But sometimes, you'll be the second one to an intersection, and Mr. Nice Guy will want to let you go first. Mr. Nice Guy might think he is being a good neighbour by letting someone go in front of him, but he is mucking up the whole system. STOP IT. These "do-gooders" are just asking for an accident, waving a hand and smiling. Your job is to sit and wait for him to comply with the rules of the four way stop. Soon, he will begin to frown and wave a hand frantically. Finally, in disgust, he will peel out and shake their fist as they go by. I hate do-gooders.

You Are Lost

If you see this sign, you are lost. Immediately turn around and consult your phone directions. Again.

How To
How to Look Busy at Work

With the ever changing economic conditions, it is imperative to keep your job. But right now, work might be slow. The boss has got her eye out for slackers. If you are lacking work around the office, your next best bet is to look like your plate is full of tasks. Here are some tips on how to look busy around the office:

Schedule all your work
I learned this as a project management tool, but it also is very helpful to make your schedule look packed. In your scheduling software, block off time for every task you have: scheduling, e-mail, meetings, returning calls, and even scheduling to send an e-mail about a returning phone calls meeting. Block off all that time. Anyone looking to schedule a meeting with you will look at your schedule and say, "Damn, he's/she's getting shit done!"

Carry stuff around
Busy people have paperwork. Busy people don't have empty hands. I suggest keeping your hands full while walking from point A to point B in the office. Even if you are taking a few sheets of paper down to the recycling bin, keep those hands full. Heck, paperclip two different piles of papers and use two hands to professionally deliver your paper to recycling. Oh, and make sure you take a few sheets OUT of the recycling bin on your way back to your desk as props. If you really want to look busy, carry a clipboard. People with clipboards are too busy to be bothered with other work. It's like a shield of protection. Hold it in front of your face for dramatic effect when someone tries to stop and talk with you.

Prop-out your desk
If your desk is neat, it might mean that you are a clean, organized worker (2% chance) or that you have nothing going on in your job (98% chance). Your desk is a great location to stage work. Keep a few files on your desk. Always keep some work in the IN box and some work in the OUT box. Leave papers with highlighter and post-its on them piled in a stack. Make sure you stamp everything with DRAFT so that people know you've got more work ahead. Half-empty coffee cups also help to sell that you are not only busy, but burning the midnight oil.

Ask about office supplies
Busy people go through things like post-it notes, DRAFT stamps and highlighters. Ask the office manager or assistant about getting more supplies or report binders. Ask your co-workers if you can steal some of their staples or binder clips. Leave an e-mail with the computer help desk that the letters on your keyboard are wearing off. Especially the P R O F I and T keys. Word will get around.

Abuse the interoffice envelope system

Busy people get internal documents. I suggest you get your hands on a few of those beautiful, yellow bastards and begin sending yourself mail from different divisions in the building. (Don't fake send documents from individuals.) Drop in a filled-out vacation form, sign HR in the FROM column and your name in the TO column. Drop in a blank check request and send it from FINANCE to yourself. Then, drop the envelopes off in other parts of the office. If the envelope does accidentally get delivered to HR or FINANCE, all they see is a form. But what should happen is that you'll receive several interoffice envelopes a day. Make sure you spread out your envelopes and exchange them with other departments so that your name doesn't appear ten times in a row.

Have lots of real mail sent to you

Busy people get snail mail. Sign up for catalogs from shipping companies or art supply distributors. Start signing up on-line for Project Management or Excel course and your mailbox will overflow with offers for 10–12 other courses in Anger Management or The Four Conversations or How to Look Busy. A full mailbox means a busy worker who shouldn't get fired.

Book a meeting room to get regular work completed

If your office is anything like mine, there are limited meeting room resources throughout most of the day. I suggest scheduling the meeting room during fringe times and use the room to get your regular work done. Sit at the table where anyone peeking in through the door will see you in there. They will assume you are running a meeting. If someone does pop in the room or if you have one of those really cool glass meeting rooms, just say that you are waiting for an outside client. If they never show up... reschedule the "meeting."

Comic
Jesus at Christmas

Hey! You just took half my Christmas gifts and put "Happy Birthday" on them!

holyjuan.com

Ask HolyJuan
Lonely on Valentine's Day

Dear HolyJuan -
Since I'm newly single and I've been reflecting on how lonely I will be this Valentine's day, I've decided to join a dating site. I have to post a sentence or phrase as a headline on my profile page. Any suggestions?

Yours truly-
single lady

Dear Single Lady,

Yeah, yeah, yeah…. Just put "I suck COCK" and you'll get 10,000 pinches or taps or winks… whatever they call it on those dating sites.

Here is what I see as the greater problem... WTF are you paying good money for to be on a dating site? And why are you single? I mean, if you suck COCK like your profile on the dating site suggested, why would your boyfriend dump you?

So instead of dating sites, let me help you find places to pick up guys on the cheap:

Bars
Guys specifically go to bars to pick up chicks. Sadly, women do not go to bars because of some issue with there being a bunch of horny guys there. BREAK THE CYCLE! Go to a bar and pick up a guy. Report your findings on the internet about how great it was to find a guy in a bar. Let's put the bra back in bar.

Church
Just kidding. Dudes you find a church are racked with guilt about the invisible man who tells them sex is bad. You don't want to date one of those guys. And plus they usually like little boys anyways.

The Internet
Get a Twitter account and tweet, "I am depressed and desperate. I live in X city. I'll be at Y bar." Boom. Done.

The Strip Club
Every guy that goes to a strip club hopes that there will be some normal girl that shows up looking for the type of greasy, sweaty, unlucky guy that they are. Find a group of guys and pick one of them (ensuring he is not the bachelor.) This will help the economy by getting more guys in the strip club in hopes that this will happen to you. Universities will see a sharp rise in income as all those strippers head to college. Then those girls will head to strip clubs to pick up guys and the circle of life will be complete.

The Olympics
No one is more vulnerable than a guy that just got 4th place in the biathlon. He'll need consoling and probably a good rub down. Stay away from the dudes way in last place. They knew they never had a chance and just take the trip to get chicks.

Columbus, OH
I understand there are a bunch of level-headed guys in Columbus, OH that will make suitable partners. While some are married, there are others that use a nom de plume and might take you out to dinner if you can make it after the kids go to bed. Do you like hot wings?

Ask HolyJuan
75 Year Old Seeks to Sell House

Dear HolyJuan,
I intend to sell my home in the spring. I am 75 and unsure about where I want to live out the rest of my days. Can you help me decide?
M

Dear M,
First off, I'm wondering if you are the 13th child of 26 with a name like M. And now I'm realizing that you are probably one of the kids of the woman who lived in a shoe that had so many children that she didn't know what to do. But she did know what to do, didn't she. She gave you watered down Lipton soup, beat you and sent you to bed so that she could watch The Voice in peace and quiet. Years have passed and now she is dead, along with your 25 brothers and sisters who died of soupafcation or athlete's foot.

And now you are left with the shoe, which you are selling.

Well, I can tell you right now that the shoe market is in a slump and there is a good chance that no one will buy it, especially after they hear that 25 kids died there. So, instead, I'm going to suggest you do not sell your house, but instead use it for making money. Here are a few ways for you to make some scratch so that you can move into one of those really nice 75 and over retirement homes where everyone sleeps around and then pretends that they "forgot" about it the next day.

Tourism
While nobody wants to buy a house that 25 kids died in, people will pay $20 a head to come tour the place. I suggest a food stand outside that sells shoe-themed foods like footlongs, sole, shoestring fries, pears? and cobbler. Once inside, give guided tours, sell audio tours and make sure the exit goes through the gift shop. In a few months, you can move into that retirement village where they have wine tastings, horseback riding and the all-you-can-eat Sociable Cracker buffet.

Raw materials
By my rough calculations, your house contains 2.5 tons of leather, 500 pounds of steel and .75 miles of woven shoestring. You could tear it down, sell it for parts and have enough money to move into a gated retirement community. Of course, the gate is to keep you in, where you will be forced to use leather and steel from a local resource to make saddles for the better retirement homes that have horseback riding.

Shoe HQ

While it didn't completely work out for Longaberger, you should try to start a shoe business out of the shoe and call it your corporate headquarters. Like I said previously, the whole thing is made out of parts that you make shoes from so you wouldn't have to go far for the shoe-making materials. You can have your offices on the laces, manufacturing in the heel, storage in the toe and you can write off your mortgage as a business expense. And once you have used every last scrap of raw materials to make shoes, sprinkle some ashes around and say the place burnt to the ground and collect insurance off of it. You'll have enough one dollar bills to keep those 75+ men busy running errands for you at the retirement boot.

Fetish

This is a huge money maker. I wouldn't suggest it, but if you look up "shoe fetish" on the internet, well, just go ahead and look it up. There are people that pay a lot of money to come over and "rent" your shoe for 30 minutes. You can host parties in there. Arrange for romantic fetish weekend getaways. You can also set up cameras throughout the shoe to capture all that goes on in there and blackmail the rich clientele. In the end, make sure that you charge enough to hire a cleaning person who specialized in protein-related leather stains.

There you have it, M., several ways for you to make some cash that you can use to put towards one of the nice retirement homes where they actually hose out the rooms once a week. Let me know how it goes and if you will have any discounts on the fetish rentals. (Asking for a friend.)

Love, HolyJuan

List
Awesome Things to Keep In Your Car Trunk

This is not going to be a list about jumper cables, a wool blanket, toilet paper and kitty litter. Your dad can tell you what items you should have in your trunk for an emergency. This list is about the other things you should have in your trunk to be Awesome.

Reflective Vest, Hard Hat and Clipboard
At some point in your life, you will want to be somewhere where you are not supposed to be. This could be a concert you don't have tickets to or into an Apple Store when there is an iPhone released. A hard hat alone will get you into 75% of places you are not supposed to be. You throw in a reflective vest and clipboard and you will most certainly be allowed to pass into any venue. The key to sneaking around is to look like you belong. Gather these items from your trunk, put them on and go through a back door or access hallway. These items not only make you look like you should be there, but you might find yourself actually running the event or changing the architecture on a major bridge project. It also works as a great Halloween costume in a pinch.

Framed, Autographed Photo of Yourself with Double Sticky Tape
Self-respecting New York delis and upstanding bars throughout the country fill their walls with autographed photos of their customers. Instead of wasting your time winning a Nobel Prize or directing a major motion film, just keep an autographed, framed photo in your trunk. Use very high bond, double sticky tape so that you don't have to bother with nails or screws. Walk in, add your face to their wall and then demand free food/drinks. If you are like me, you keep several framed photos in the car with a sharpie so that the photo can be personalized to the location.

A Roll of Toilet Paper
OK. So I lied about the toilet paper. But I'm not talking about emergency craps on the side of the Interstate between the car door and your embarrassed spouse holding a jacket to hide your shame. I've got something more nefarious in mind. We all have an enemy. If you don't, get one. It's great to focus your own personal failings on someone else. Late at night, when you are driving past your enemy's house, jump out and use that one roll of toilet paper to TP a tree/shrub. You don't have to use the whole roll. Just get a good foundation going and then leave the rest of roll. The next morning, your enemy will walk out and see this attack upon their homestead. They are going to think two things:

1. They have been attacked and they don't know why.

2. The attack was halted, as only one roll was partially used, and the perpetrators will be back to finish the job.

You now have created a paranoid enemy. They'll constantly be looking over their shoulder. They'll stay up late at night, hiding in the bushes with a shotgun, waiting to take out the next person who steps in their yard. Over time, they'll become exhausted, go crazy and get arrested for shooting the paper delivery girl. Then it's time for you to get another roll of toilet paper and a new enemy.

Two Sets of Jumper Cables
OK. So I lied about the jumper cables. Here's the deal. Anyone asking you for a jumpstart is really at the bottom of the barrel. They don't have AAA. They knew their battery was shitty and they didn't replace it. They don't have friends because otherwise they wouldn't be asking you. On top of that... they don't even have jumper cables. Their life sucks. But you are Awesome and you come to their rescue. You give them the jump they need to get their car started. And on top of that... you GIVE them your 2nd set of jumper cables. Let's be honest... if their car has died once, it's going to die again. They'll need those jumper cables. Plus, it will leave a lifelong impression on them, just like it did to me.

Comic
Jesus at the Summer Olympics

Collection
College Pranks

For a few quarters in college, I lived in an apartment with two high school buddies, Nick and Doug. When we first moved in, we drew straws to see what order we would pick rooms. Doug won. Nick got second and I got third. I was doomed to get the smallest room that was awkwardly shaped with the fuse box on the wall. Doug changed all that when he picked the worst room for himself. Nick picked second and got the best room and I got the second best room. Doug stood by his choice and I'll never know what he saw in that room.

It wasn't long until Nick and I started pulling pranks on each other. Doug didn't want any part of our pranks, but accidentally became an integral part.

Nick had a waterbed. On one long weekend in the winter, Nick left for two days and so I left his window open, unplugged his waterbed heater and covered all his vents with towels. The hope was to get the waterbed to freeze. It didn't freeze, but it took several days for the small heater to get back to normal temperature.
Score– Me: 1, Nick: 0.

One night, when Doug and I had gone out drinking, Nick tried to get me back by engineering a complex "bucket over the door" device in my room made of cardboard, string, tape and the with the help of four or five German beers he had brought from home. When Doug and I got back from a night of drinking, Nick was acting odd and kept asking me to walk into my room. Doug grew tired of me questioning Nick's motives and walked in first and... nothing happened. Somewhere between the 3rd and 4th German beer, Nick's engineering skills failed him. The bucket of water stayed in its cardboard nest. If it had worked, Doug would have been doused. Instead, Nick was required to curse physics and angrily dismantle it.
Score: Me: 1, Nick: -1.

A few weeks after the failed bucket of water gag, Nick took my mattress off my bed, put it in the shower, and re-made it. He did a damn good job tucking the sheets in and stuffing the pillow so that it would stick. Doug made it home before me and went into the bathroom. Even though you could not really see the mattress through the mostly opaque shower curtain, you could sense its presence. It was creepy. Doug completely freaked out. I think he got the broom out and was poking at the shower curtain while yelling at it to see who was behind it.
Score: Me: 1, Nick: -1/2.

This is when I decided to pull off The Grand Prank. A multi-level puzzle full of trickery. I had to wait for the perfect time and Nick gave it to me when he went back to Lancaster for the afternoon, but was coming back later that evening. Here's what I did:

Step One: Bring On the Noise
I took the looping cassette tape out of our answering machine. Back in the day, phone answering machines had two cassette tapes in them; one normal tape for recording messages and one looping tape that was 30 seconds long. You would record your message on the 30 second tape and it would loop around to the beginning for the next call. The answering machine could detect when the tape looped and would stop it. A regular tape player would not recognize the cue and it would play the tape endlessly. I recorded my voice on the tape saying, "I got you this time, Nick. Ha ha ha ha. I got you this time, Nick Ha ha ha ha ha." I put this tape in my stereo that was in my bedroom and blasted it.

Step Two: Lock Down
My room was only slightly wider than the length of my bed. So I angled the bed in front of the door just enough so that I could squeeze out. Then I used a metal coat hanger to pull the bed against the door to wedge the door shut. If you pushed against the door, it would only open about three inches wide and I positioned the tape player half way across the room and way out of reach. To get the door open, you would need to use something like a yard stick under the door to push the bed out from behind the door. We had a beautiful, quarter inch thick yardstick that would work perfectly for this and so I hid it in the couch.

Step Three: Plot Twist!
Nick was a smart guy. Once he realized he wouldn't be able to get into my room, he would head straight to the fuse box. Our fuse box was in Doug's room and the fuses weren't labeled. To be deceptive, I put several layers of tape over one of the fuses. Then I took a wooden coat hanger and screwed it to the wall next to the one fuse to keep it from being turned on. It would take a bit of doing to get that stuff off, especially after I hid the drill and tools. The item I failed to mention is that the fuse I covered was not the fuse to my room. Anyone looking at that fuse box would assume it was the right fuse and take the time to uncover it.

Step Four: Lights Out
Finally, on my way out, I removed every single bulb in the house and hid them in the linen closet under the extra towels. (Yeah, we actually had extra towels. Nick and Doug ran a tight ship.)

I left for the night, knowing I would be staying at Johnny Two-Sack's place. In the morning I would come back to a very pissed off, but hopefully proud Nick.
When I rolled in the next afternoon, there was no Nick to be found, only one very angry Doug.

Nick hadn't come home that night. Nick ended up staying in Lancaster for the evening and playing golf the next day. But Doug had. Doug said he came home from a night of "partying" and stood in the doorway for about five minutes trying to figure out what the hell was going on. None of the lights would work. Something loud was playing in my bedroom. After stumbling though the apartment, Doug tried to open my door and it wouldn't budge. It only opened about three inches. He reached his arm through the door and…
…turned off the light switch. The same light switch that also controlled the outlet that the stereo was plugged into. The player went off. Doug crawled into his dark room and went to bed.

So I had to clean up the mess. I wanted to leave everything the way it was, but I had to get the power back on to the living room (the actual fuse I had off,) replace all the light bulbs and at some point I would need to get back in my bedroom. Nick came home late on Sunday. He had decided to stay home all of Friday and play golf on Saturday. He ending up unknowingly pranking me.

He asked how the weekend went. I said it was great.
Score– Doug: 0 Nick: 0

How To
How to Answer a Child's Questions About Death

Right after sex and the alt-right movement, death is one of the most difficult matters to explain to a child. Here are some questions you may get and some sample answers in reference to a dead Uncle Bob. Remember, the name you use may be different, so do not read these word for word to the child unless your dead person is named Bob.

1. Where's Uncle Bob?
Uncle Bob is dead.

2. What is dead?
Dead is when you stop breathing.

3. I can hold my breath.
That is not a question, but I'll answer it anyways. If you were to hold your breath for a long time you would die. Just like Uncle Bob.

4. Is Uncle Bob being punished by God?
No. Uncle Bob did not believe in God. Too bad for Bob, because God believed in him. So now Bob is in hell with the devil and eternal fires.

5. Why is Bob in that box?
Bob is in that plain box because he could not afford the metal one with the stainless steel. Bob was a bad planner and spent his money on booze and women. Daddy wishes he could have the plain box.

6. No, why is he in that box and not moving?
He's dead. I thought we covered that in #1.

7. No, why is he out so we can see him?
Uncle Bob is being displayed so that people can say their last good-byes. In a little while, they will shut the box and bury the box in the ground.

8. Why do we put people in the ground?
Dead people can come back as zombies and it is best to lock them up and stick them as far as possible under the earth. Remember, only a head shot can take out a zombie. Don't try to light them on fire. You can also hit them with a guitar.

9. Mom said Uncle Bob was going to be cremated.

Oh shit. You are right. He'll get stuffed in the flames, crackle, crackle, crackle, then they give us a handful of ashes, which we can pretend are his.

10. Was that last line a complete rip off from the Monty Python "Undertaker" sketch?
Yes. Your Uncle Bob loved Python. And scotch.

11. What are all these rocks with the writing on them?
Those are called tombstones. They are overpriced chunks of marble so that we can remember that we outlived Uncle Bob. You'll note that Uncle Bob's tombstone looks like everyone else's and we are bound to spend countless hours searching around for it so that your mother can swap out the flowers.

12. Why is everyone crying?
Uncle Bob owed a lot of people a lot of money. This funeral ain't cheap either.

13. You didn't like Uncle Bob, did you?
It's not polite to say bad things about the dead.

14. Will I die?
Someday, yes. But not for a long time. You'll spend years of your life, trudging and plodding and scraping by. You'll get married and have kids and retire. Then one day you'll ask yourself "why?" Then you'll impatiently wait for death to come to your doorstep.

15. Which is harder to explain: death, sex or neo-conservatism?
Sex, then neo-conservatism and then death. In that order.

16. Why do people have to die?
People have to die so that the cigarette companies can make more money. At least that's what I read somewhere.

17. Did Bonkers die?
No, Bonkers ran away. And let's stick with the Uncle Bob theme.

18. What if Uncle Bob wakes up and he is under ground?
Good question. Uncle Bob is really, really dead. But just in case, all bodies are buried with a cell phone and five free minutes. I hope this cemetery isn't outside of our calling area.

19. Are you going to try to stretch this out to an even twenty questions?
No.

Comic
Jesus in the Shower

The drain is stopped up again.

holyjuan.com

List
10 Phone Numbers to Sneak Into Your Friend's Phone

What would you do if your friend accidentally left their cell phone at your house or possibly on the restaurant table when they headed for the bathroom? I suggest editing their cell phone contacts list. The following list can be added to their contacts or you can take their existing entries like HOME or MOM and update them with a number from this list.

The White House - 202-456-1414
This number works as a great replacement for the HOME number. If your friend calls it really drunk one night, they'll either get, "Mr. Biden, do we need to send a car for you?" or "Damnit George, quit calling this number."

North American Man/Boy Love Association (NAMBLA) - 212-631-1194
NAMBLA works best as a phone list entry on its own. Girls have a tendency to secretly check potential boyfriend's phones for other girl's numbers. If you have had several girls run for the door on the first date, you should probably check your own phone. If they see this in your phone and decide to stick around, YOU should run for the door.

FBI - 202-324-3000
The FBI phone number makes a good replacement number for someone you do not like in your friend's cell phone address book. Then you can call them out as a government stooge and make it back to the top of the friend list.

National Herpes Hotline - 919-361-8488
Another good number to add as-is. What really can stink about this one is when you add it and the phone tells you, "Number all ready exists in memory." In that case, put down the phone and wash your hands with Valtrex.

Aesthetic Plastic Surgery International - 703-845-7400
Aesthetic Plastic Surgery International is world renown for their penis enlargement skills and breast augmentation. Use this number under your friend's current listing for "Doctor" or even better, "Dentist."

Suicide Hotline - 1-800-273-8255
An oldie, but goodie. See if you can exchange this number for whatever your friend has under their #2 speed dial. OR if they have just been dumped, enter the number as is. They might need it.

Scientology - 323-960-3500
Careful with this number. I would recommend using this number with a fake name like John Travolta or Tom Cruise.

One Night Stand Hotline - 212-201-3517
Your friend rushes home to tell you about that perfect person they met at the bar and went home and had six hours of unbelievable unicorn sex with. They pass out from drink and love. You update that new number with this one and the next day when they call, they get a high pitched recording of some dude telling them they've been one night standed. Classic!

Green Door Swinger's Club in Vegas – 702-732-4656
This is the number one phone number to stick in your friend's phone as-is. Once they find it and do an internet search on what the Green Door is, they will re-label the phone number as "Stacy EnVegas" hoping one day to call it as a local number.

World of Warcraft Support Line - 800-592 5499
What's great about this number is that I'm not sure if support means "Did you forget your password" or "Just lie down and tell me how it all started back in Necromancer school."

BONUS NUMBER - 614-GAY-IDOL
Just because I like getting phone calls in the middle of the night asking for directions to the audition.

Comic
Vacuum

How To
How to Tell if a Woman is Crazy

Despite what you may believe, most women are not crazy. In fact, they probably have their shit together more than you. But for those of you who do find yourself in a situation with a woman who you think might be a whack job, here's how you can tell.

Hair past her ass
Super long hair is a dead giveaway. Either she's a religious nut or just has WAY too much time to wash and dry it. No woman should spend that much time on her hair just to straighten out the split ends. And nothing says stay away like a six foot long, fat-ass braid. Here's a good rule of thumb: if she can strangle you with it, it's too long.

Wants sex all the time
Every guy dreams about it, but you never hear about anyone surviving it. 98% of sex is convincing a woman to sleep with your unhealthy, hairy ass. If she wants it all the time, it's no longer a challenge, and you stop wanting it. Then she starts to accuse you of cheating, shortly after which comes the Phil Hartman afternoon dirt nap.

Crazy eyes or never blinks
If you can see the entire pupil plus a good bit of white around it, she's crazy. If she doesn't ever blink, that's not right. If she blinks all the time, that's just as screwed up. It's sexy if one eye is a different color, but if she has a glass eye with no pupil, check her for a knife and duck out the back door.

Talks about husband in the past tense
It's a good idea to stay away from married women. It's a really good idea to get as far away as possible from soon-to-be widows.

Doesn't talk
You may think it is sexy for a woman at a party to stare you down across the room, walk over and grab your hand, lead you to an empty bedroom and blow you. I guarantee the reason she is not talking is because she doesn't have any teeth or she doesn't have any vagina. Trust me, most transgender dudes don't have much to say... on the first date.

Smokes Capris
Trust me. Crazy.

She's Conservative
No woman should be Conservative. It just ain't right. Conservative woman have to be subservient to their husbands, and no woman should have to do that. Let's face it, you'd have to be completely f*cking crazy to let a man run your life.

Has kids, but never mentions them
Every non-crazy woman is in love with her kids. A cheating woman will still lie in bed with her cheat and talk about her kids. If a woman is silent about her kids, it's because her brakes are about to fail near a river. Avoid.

Drinks vodka tonic without tonic
I like a woman that drinks. I don't like a woman that can drink more than me. If she's drinking straight from a bottle, you'd best stay away. Also be on the lookout for any woman who has a whole box of wine in the fridge and is brewing beer in a bag in the basement.

Laughs. All the time.
Most funny women are at least half-crazy. Women shouldn't have to tell jokes to get attention because they have boobs for that. If a woman tells jokes to get laughs, she's mostly crazy. If all she does is laugh and especially in a barking laugh, she's just plain crazy. But now that I think about it, I'd rather deal with a crazy woman than a half crazy one. At least with a crazy woman, you know what you're getting into. There's something to be said for predictability.

Comic
Jesus Plays Ball

The baseball game is off, Jesus. We are short three players.

No, problem.

I went over to the cemetery.

holyjuan.com

Collection
Jesse Jackson is Human

At one point in my life, I thought I was going to be a weatherman. I went to Ohio University and applied to the Scripps School of Journalism so that I could get into broadcast news. Due to my pathetic grammar skills, I failed the English exam (twice) and had to transfer to the Telecommunications School to get a degree in Video Production. Who would have ever thought that if I had not failed that English test, that I might have missed out on the opportunity to hear Rev. Jesse Jackson fart.

Part of the Telecommunications experience at OU is the internship program. My internship was at Lyon Video in Columbus, Ohio and it was an awesome experience. I got to learn everything about video production, smoke, drink, hang out with aspiring local E List actors and pretend like the company was going to hire me on full time after graduation.

In the fall of 1992, the Presidential election was eating up all the network time. Clinton was taking on Bush and SNL was having a ball with Perot. In Columbus, Rev. Jesse Jackson was passing through town, drumming up votes for Bill. The BET network threw together a last minute Town Hall Meeting and Lyon Video was asked to host the event.

In Studio A, I helped to set up about 200 chairs as a small stage was constructed towards the front of the studio. An aspiring journalist practiced her questions to Mr. Jackson. This was her big chance. This was going to catapult her career through the alphabet from BET to NBC. The stage was staged. The lights were lit. The cameras were cameraing. People started to enter the studio.

About 40 people that is.

For some reason, Columbus couldn't scrape together 200 people to see Jesse Jackson. It was a last minute event, but heck, even the MacGyver Fan Club could throw together 200 people in four hours. We removed a bunch of chairs from the studio and arranged the rest so that the studio would look full in the eye of the camera. Jesse's people were yelling at the local Democratic Party members. It was a grand occasion.

It was a really grand occasion because someone decided that I should floor direct. The floor director wears a big headset and gets to yell "Five minutes people!" and "Thirty seconds 'till air!" You also get to hold up five fingers and decrease them all the way down until two fingers and then you use the last finger to point. Sometimes you even get to hold cue cards. Sadly, we used a teleprompter so I wasn't able to misspell Clinton on the cards.

Jesse came in and sat down. Jesse is a big dude. He's tall. He's a bit thick, too.

I used the finger pointy at the host trick and we were off. The interviewer asked questions and Jesse answered them. I can't remember what was said because I was busy listening to the banter in the booth and pointing at the different cameras. After a break the reporter took questions from audience members. At this point, I was able to saddle up next to camera one and hang out. The reporter was floating in the audience and there was no need for me to whip out my pointy finger. On stage, Jesse was showing some wear. He'd been putting in some long days and he seemed uncomfortable as he was sweating under the lights. The reporter threw a question at Jesse and he began to answer. In mid-sentence he uncrossed his legs and began to re-cross them.

Frrrrrt.

Now, I'm not sure how you spell it where you come from, but in Ohio, we spell a ¾ second fart with solid bi-gluteus vibration like this, "Frrrrrt." You western folk may throw a "V" in there – "Vrrrrrt." I hear tell southern people don't spell the word because you can't see a fart. They just leave empty space, " ."

Either way, Jesse farted. Over the headset the audio guy said, "What was that?" The camera guy next to me held back 95% of a laugh. Murdock, all the way down at camera three, looked directly at me and mouthed the words, "Did he fart?" The audio guy spoke up again, "I think he just farted." I answered in the most straight faced of whispers, "Yes he did." The whole booth cracked up laughing. The camera guys held it together because they could hide their smirks in the viewfinders of the cameras. I was stuck out in the open and had to kneel down in the Floor Director pose #8 to regain my composure. The interview continued.

So, Rev. Jesse Jackson is human. And he's actually more human than that.

When the event was over, the audio guy went into the green room to fetch the wireless mic off of Jesse. He came out with eyes wide and reported that when he walked into the room, Jesse had a Wendy's chicken sandwich open in his hands. Jesse was looking down at the mayo and lettuce and tomato side and said, "Who's been f*cking with my sandwich? Somebody's been f*cking with my sandwich." I couldn't believe it. No way. Not a Reverend! I didn't believe it and I'm sure he was lying.

That was until I heard Jesse respond to one of his entourage. The guy was walking Jesse towards the exit and I was following. The entourage guy informed Jesse that the Dems were hosting a party at a local hotel and they wanted him to come over. Jesse replied frankly, "I don't want to go to any f*cking party. I'm tired." And they left.

As far as I'm concerned, Jesse is all right in my book. Heck, if he can complete the trifecta of farting, cussing and drinking PBR, he could almost be considered a native of Ohio.

So, cheers for my crappy grammar. And thanks for the internship Bob Lyon. And here's to the White Castles that Jesse ate in the car on the way to the studio. Thanks for the story, Mr. Jackson.

Ask HolyJuan
Neighbors Park on Our Side of the Street

Dear Holy Juan,

I have a little dilemma that needs to be handled with tact.

Our new neighbours keep parking their car in front of our house. We both have garages. We both have driveways. We both have the same amount of curb space. But they put their car in front of our house. They park in such a way that it takes up the space where two cars could fit. Of course, it also blocks our view, and our guests are forced to park far away.

Well, of course, our guests could park in front of their house. I've told a few friends to do this. They said our neighbors were outside at the time and glared at them as they got out of the car and walked over to our house.

I don't know what action to take. I thought of leaving a note, but I don't know what to say.

These neighbors are new to this country, and they kind of keep to themselves. I don't want to cause offense. I just want them to move their car!

--- Kristen

Dear --- Kristen,

I have a plan.

I'm assuming that your new neighbours are French because they sound like real assholes.

You may want a pen to write this down. Or I guess you could just print it.

First, you will need to get a cat. If you have one, great. If you do not, even better because cats are horrible pets. I have two and I would give you both of them for this if I had the chance. So, if you do not have a cat, borrow one.

Now, you are going to need to find a dead cat that looks like your cat / your borrowed cat. They are all over the place so just get a cooler, some dry ice and put the dead cat in the cooler for transportation back to your freezer. Make sure it's really dead or you'll be really mad at yourself when that little f*cker leaps out of the cooler and tears your eyes out.

Next, you'll want to go to the neighbor's house with the live cat in hand. Knock on the door and tell them that you saw them almost run over your cat when they parked in front of your house. Ask them if they would park on their side to avoid killing your cat. At this point, if they truly are French, they will ignore you.

The next time they park in your spot, thaw out the dead cat in the microwave (you may want to put some paper towels down) and then put the dead cat under their front wheel. Make sure you take lots of photos. Then go to their door and accuse them of killing your cat.

When they go to examine the dead cat, hit the red button on the remote control that detonates the explosive charge that you hid inside the dead cat's body. Hopefully you'll have used enough C4 to both kill the car owner and blow the car over on to their side of the street.

My work here is done.

Best of luck with the Frenchies!

Comic
Jesus' Gym

List
Numbers and Time: A Child's View

Children have a very different sense of numbers and time. Here is a refresher course for you on both.

Kids' math might be a little bit off, but they have a greater understanding of what numbers actually mean. Here is a list of numbers and what kids think of them:

None
There is no such thing as none to a child. If there is none, they ask for more and they will continue to ask and ask for more until none is gone.

Half
Unless it is a kid's birthday, they will always tack this number on to the tail end of whatever their age is. The fun part is watching kids try to make "half" while holding up their fingers.

One
When a kid says "one" it is always followed up by the word "more." Once parents introduce television or videogames into their child's life, "one" is then followed up by "more minute."

Two
Two is the magical number. Two is how many minutes kids' parents trick them into thinking they have left to play. It's a good trick because it works by setting up an expectation and doesn't force the child to quit what they are doing immediately. In reality, two minutes can mean one minute because kids forget or ten minutes because parents forget.

Three
Three is the never number. Children hear that they have until the count of three and the parent never gets past counting two and a half or two and nine tenths.

Five
Five is the trickiest number. Five is what we set kids up for as the greatest number in the world because at five they get to go to kindergarten. Kids wait for five. Then they go to kindergarten and wonder what the big deal was.

Kids know a lot less about time. Here's what they do know:

Right now
Right now means that the kid should have stopped doing what they are doing about five seconds ago. The kid hopes at this point that their kid brain quits what they are doing so that they don't hear the follow up, very dangerous single word, "Now!"

Now
You are in trouble. You should have listened when it was "right now."

A week
A week is FOREVER. They might as well curl up and die.

The rest of your life
This is how long kids get to feel guilty for not listening or breaking something. At least until they have kids and can pass the guilt on to them. Later, this is replaced by "permanent record."

Six weeks
This is how long stuff kids send in for takes to show up. And usually it's not as big or as x-rayish as anyone thought it would be.

Next year
Next year sucks because it means that they didn't get what they wanted this year and their parent are rubbing their hair, trying to make them feel better and using the word "kiddo" a lot.

Never
Never is the harshest word that kids learn is meaningless the second time it is used. Parent use never all the time and do not follow through. Kids pick up on this and when they hear never, they know they can just wait it out.

Tomorrow
Tomorrow is the greatest time of all. Tomorrow is not today. Tomorrow is full of candy and sunshine and play. If today sucks, there's always tomorrow. And when today is good, there's a chance that tomorrow will be even better.

Comic
Morning Math

Definition: Morning Math

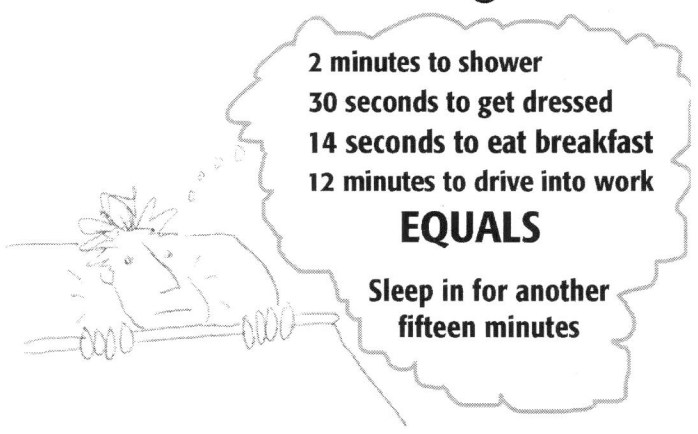

2 minutes to shower
30 seconds to get dressed
14 seconds to eat breakfast
12 minutes to drive into work
EQUALS
Sleep in for another fifteen minutes

While lying in bed deciding when to get up, the times you use in your calculations are your personal best.

holyjuan.com

How To
How to Leave a Party Early

As soon as you are invited to one party and you accept the initiation, inevitably, a better offer comes around. There is an art to leaving a party early without offending your host. Here's how you do it.

1. The BEST way to leave is just to leave. Don't say good-bye. Don't tell anyone. Just leave. You will not be missed. The next day if the host asks you why you left, claim that you got into an intense discussion with a person whose name you cannot remember and that you left about ten minutes after X person puked. If the host says that X person didn't puke, laugh and say, "Oh crap, they told me to promise that I wouldn't tell."

2. Ask the host for Imodium AD. Ten minutes later excuse yourself. No questions asked.

3. Ask the host if you can lie down in a spare bedroom. Use the jackets on the bed to make a fake you under the covers. If the host looks in, they'll see a fake you. When guests leave, they'll take their jackets and you will have disappeared without having to make an excuse.

4. Ask the host if they have a really, really expensive brand of wine. (I don't know any myself, but ask for a late 90's six syllable French sounding something and it will pass. Start with Château Château and you'll be fine.) When your host says no, say you are going to run out and grab a bottle. Call from wherever you are at later and say you are still searching for it. Next day, leave a bottle of wine on their porch with a note saying, "Found it!"

5. Browse the snacks. Get a dip or white sauce that might have milk in it. Walk up to the host with the bowl and say, "This soy dip is awesome!" When they correct you and say that the item is milk based, get all wide eyed, cover your mouth and run for the door.

6. If all else fails, be honest and truthful with your host. Walk right up to them, take a deep breath and tell them your mother just called and that your father has had a massive heart attack and you must leave. If this is your second party you are bailing on, make sure mom is having the heart attack this time.

List
Reasons Why The Idiot In Front of You Can't Drive
I know you know how to drive just fine, but the asshole in front of you has no idea what the hell he's doing. Here's why:

1. Mirrors aren't positioned right
Mirrors should be adjusted to eliminate blind spots. A passing car should be visible in the driver's rear view mirror and before it disappears, it should be visible in the side view mirror and then in a driver's peripheral vision before it leaves the side view mirror. Most people adjust their side mirror to see if they've left the gas flap open and then leave it there.

2. Doesn't look through cars
Most cars have a good bit of glass in them. In most states, that glass has to be clear. What this means is a driver can look through the cars around them to see stuff. That's right! Right through it. If they are turning left and the guy next to them is too much of a wimp to turn, they don't have to wait for him, they just need to look though his car and see if traffic is clear. This helps with passing, too.

Fuzzy dice are a problem with this theory. Fat heads too, which is why not a lot of people pass me.

3. Doesn't know how to yield
On ramps are launch pads. By the halfway point of the on ramp, a driver should be doing the speed limit, which I think is around 75. Yield does not mean "be a bitch," it means playing a game of chicken with the driver they are about to hit. This continues until the mergee backs down or they merger give in and slides in behind him at the last second. Many idiots get up to 50% of the speed limit and start looking backwards at the traffic. Then they hit the brakes. If drivers do as I suggest, they will be at 75 MPH at this point and should pass them on the median.

4. Not a team player
Here is the biggest problem that idiot drivers have: they forget that this is a team effort. If there is a line of 50 cars at a stop light, the 50th guy has a chance to make it through if we all work together. The whole team is expecting that the #1 car has his shit together and will lead the team to victory. #1 car should be watching the cross traffic light. If they look close, they can see it change to yellow and then red. On yellow, the driver should take their foot off the brake as this will cue car #2 which will cue car #3 and so on. Watch the light turn red and make sure no one is going to run it. As soon as it is green, hit it. Don't f*ck around. Gogogogogogogogo!! Of those 50 cars, the first 25 can make it though in the first eight seconds. All cars need to commit! No slamming on the brakes if they get nervous, the team is counting on them! The last car through should be in the middle of the intersection when the light turns red. A team effort, people.

5. Sucks at left turns
I drove in Boston for about four months and the one thing I learned is that the car turning left always shoots through the intersection as soon as the light turns green. I am cool with this. It might piss off the car coming straight through the intersection, unless they expect it, which all drivers should. The second car in line should drive 49.9999% of the way into the intersection, almost nose to nose with the car doing the same on the other side. Drivers just need a bit of space to complete the turn. The second car in line to turn left should be on the #1 cars ass. #3 car should do the same. When the light turns red, all three cars go. Just watch out for the car in cross traffic trying to get the jump on the left turn.

6. Speeds up when you try to pass
While idiot driver is going 53–56 MPH on the highway, a normal driver might decide pass him. This is a challenge to idiot driver and they'll speed up. I notice this all the time on my way to work because I slap the cruise control on for the first half of the trip and I am very aware of how fast I am going. My passing might as

well be a reminder to the idiot driver that his genitals are still very small and he'll take it out on his accelerator. Usually, they speed up just enough to match the passing driver's speed. I've found that, within reason, speeding up and getting past them is enough to dampen their aggression and as soon as they see the bumper, they will slow back down to their widely fluctuating speed until they are passed again. That is unless it's to get a better shot at you though your rear window.

7. Going straight in the right hand lane
Rights on red are legal in my state. If they aren't in yours, you should move. Nonetheless, idiot driver in front of you wants to be the first guy at the light so he'll stray from the left lane to block the right so that you cannot turn right. This is a dick move. They should stay in the left lane, even if there is an opening.

8. Sucks at passing
When an idiot driver passes, they'll maintain their speed, even if it is .03 MPH faster than the car they are passing. It could take 12 days to pass at that rate. When a driver passes another vehicle, they should get a pair and pass it... now! They should make it their mission to get around that slower vehicle as fast as possible and then pull over and resume their crappy pre-pass speed.

9. On your ass
(I realize this detracts from the "Idiot In Front of You" theme, but stick with me, it's the last one.) I keep my distance behind the car in front of me because I do not want to ride up his ass when he slams on his brakes for a kitty cat crossing the street. Idiot driver behind thinks that somehow a driver will speed up if he rides their ass. This is just not cool and does not work into the whole team work theory we spoke of earlier. Drivers should back a couple car lengths. I have learned a trick where I step on the brake pedal with my left foot just enough to trigger the brake light, but not trigger the brakes. That usually freak them the hell back.

10. Does any of the following
Throws shit out the window
Makes out with girlfriend*
Can't handle road head
Can't find a CD under the seat
Doesn't know how to talk and drive
Is out of windshield wiper fluid (guilty)
Is missing a mirror(guilty)
Smokes a pipe
Eats a foot long sub (guilty)
Masturbating (also guilty)

*To end this article, I tell you a story I swear is true: on my way home on the highway one fine evening, I witnessed a car swerving and sped up to see what the hell was going on. In the driver's seat sat a female. The passenger seat there was a male. The male leaned over and grabbed the steering wheel and the driver leaned over and, I assume, BEGAN TO BLOW THE PASSENGER. The car continued down the highway with the dude leaning over, swerving every so often. This continued for six or seven minutes, even as they transitioned between the highway and the outer belt, until the girl popped up and they pulled off an exit ramp.

For reasons which you may be aware, I have always called this Postal Head and think about it whenever I travel down 670.

Comic
Ikalvery

Collection
I Got My Hair Cut at the Black Barber Shop

I couldn't be much whiter. For example, I get my hair cut at Great Clips. For another, I do my best to pretend that I'm not the least bit racist.

My wife, Miss Sally, and I were surprised one Saturday morning when we pulled up to the local Great Clips and it was shut down. I really needed a haircut and sadly, Great Clips is where I get that done. I remembered there was a barber shop around the corner in the strip mall, so we drove over there. I knew it had to be a barber shop because it said, "Donnie's Barber Salon" on the sign and there was a barber pole spinning thing on the outside. You can't go wrong with the spinning blue, red and white pole. That means barber shop.

We walked in and immediately noticed the lack of whiteness. The barber was black. The customer in the chair was black. The guy hanging out and reading a magazine in the other barber chair was black. And we were getting paler by the second.

The magazine guy in the chair took one look at us and stood up. He apologized, "I don't cut hair," and sat in one of the waiting chairs. The barber said hello. I asked if I could get a haircut and he said yes. We sat down.

I made the decision not to leave. My instincts told me to leave, but I told my instincts to stuff it. I wasn't going to let my ignorance get the better of me. I shouldn't be worried about a hair cut from a black man. The guy was a barber and barbers cut hair. Hair is hair, right?

The Vibe magazine I picked up was at least six months old. I pretended to be interested in an article about P. Diddy. Miss Sally excused herself and went around the corner to go get a few things at the Rite-Aid.

Holy shit if cutting black guy's hair doesn't take a long time. The barber was detailing the customer's head with a determined precision. I think at one point he used a protractor to get top just so. This barber was good.

I had a Caucasian sigh of relief when another white guy walked in. He was a big dude with a definite brother charm. The guys in the barber shop warmly welcomed him. The not-barber stood up and gave the white guy a hand grasp which was then used as a man shield to fill the void between them when they did a quick hug. The white dude asked if he could get cleaned up. The man who wasn't a barber suddenly remembered that he was actually a barber and had the guy sit in the second chair. I was just about to be offended when the non-barber black guy became a barber pulled out the clippers and took white guy's hair down a sandpaper thickness with a few quick passes over his scalp. It was a shearing, not a haircut.

White guy left and I waited.

The barber finally finished up with his customer and called me over. I sat down in the chair and the barber asked me how I wanted to get my hair cut. I told him the standard, "#4 on the sides and scissor cut on top. I like to part my hair." What happened next was a haircut that can only be compared to the awkwardness of a one fingered teenage boy trying to open a bra for the first time. The barber got out his scissors and started cutting my hair on top first. This was new to me. The chicks at Great Clips use the trimmer first on the sides and then move to the scissors. There was a lot of clipping and pausing and more clipping. Of course, I wasn't going to say anything. This guy was a barber. A professional.

At one point the barber moved around to the front and I noticed his hands. His hands were covered with hairs. Other men's hairs. What looked to be the hair from 1,000 men. Little tiny bits of straight and curly black hairs. There were no white guy hairs yet.

Miss Sally returned to the barbershop with her purchases and sat down. I think she was amazed that I was still there. She had been gone about forty five minutes. She, too, feigned interest in P. Diddy.
The clippers came out, but only for a minute and then back to the scissoring. He started to get exasperated, combing my hair over and cutting. Stopping. Staring. Tentative cutting again. I finally stopped him and said, "That's good. That's fine." The barber literally shrugged his shoulders and mumbled what sounded like an apology. I waited for him to remove the hair cloak from my neck when there was a clink of a bottle and two man hands rubbing my hair. I hadn't asked for gel, but just wanted to get out of there and… wait… what's that smell? Coconut? I reached up and felt my hair… it was oily and coconutty. Barber put coconut oily something in my hair. I'm not sure what the product is supposed to do, but if the bottle said "Pisses Off White Boys" then shit, it was working.

I stood up and looked in the mirror. I looked like a wet dog with a bad haircut. I paid him. He gave back my change and I held out $5 for a tip. He said, "No. You don't have to." I gritted a smile and said, "No, take it." He did. We left.

I steamed silently the entire ride back home. Oily something dripped down my neck. I showered as soon as I stomped in the house. Small black hairs flecked the shower floor. We drove to the Great Clips across town. The lady asked if I had tried to cut my own hair.

Perhaps I should have better communicated with the barber about my concerns or directed him on how I wanted my hair cut. Or maybe he should have told me that he didn't cut white people hair. Neither one of us wanted to offend the other. Both of us ended up feeling foolish. Though I was the only one who looked foolish.

Comic
Jesus' Shadow

How To
How to Show Up Late to Work, Leave Early and Get Away With It

It's easy to show up late to work and leave early if you follow these simple tips.

Clandestine Closet
You'll need to find a closet near the front door or secret side door where you can hide "late" supplies and hang your jacket. I suggest keeping a stack of papers or some blue prints in there. When you slide in late, hang up your coat so that people don't see you with your jacket on. Grab a stack of stuff and complain about the Gibson account to whomever you see.

Computer On
Always leave your computer and monitor on. Disable the screen saver or make your screen saver a full sized image of an Excel spreadsheet. Make sure you keep several programs open. I know I'm going to Environmental Hell for this one, but a few dollars of electricity a week is totally worth the extra sleep you will get.

Double Coats/Sweatshirts
When you leave work at night (or hopefully in the early afternoon) leave a spare jacket or sweatshirt on the back of your chair. Turn the chair slightly out as if you just stood up and plan to come back. If you're leaving early, people will think you are coming back. If you are showing up late, people will think you've beaten them to the office and are at an early meeting. This especially works well if your computer is on.

Call Your Desk Phone and Hang Up After One Ring
If your co-workers hear your phone ringing off the hook, they will know you are not at your desk. When you leave early for the day, call in to your desk and hang up. With a subliminal one or two rings every twenty minutes, your boss will think you are answering calls and running errands, you multi-tasker you!

Office Pool
If you are just rolling in at 10:00 a.m. and need to trick your boss into thinking that you have been in the office all morning, utilize the Office Pool. Get a box top from some copier paper and throw whatever change and bills you have in it. Make sure you have a pen and piece of paper with writing on it (bonus points for a clipboard.) Pop in your boss' office and tell him you are collecting money for Betty in Custodial

pregnancy and that he is the last one on the list. Your boss will pretend like they know about Betty's bastard child and wish her the best. "Check" his name off the list and say you will give your best to Betty. Spend boss' cash later that afternoon at the bar with a toast to Betty's soon-to-be-announced and soon-to-be-office-pool-money-collected miscarriage.

Copier Problems
Having a small bag of toner around can be useful for staging a "copier blow-up." As you get into work, rub some on your face and sprinkle some on your hidden stash of papers. Make sure you ask if anyone has seen the copier guy. You can spend hours searching for the right "Drum and Blade Kit."

Trick Away E-mail
Your e-mail probably has an "away" setting in which a return e-mail message is sent out during times when you are on an actual vacation. I suggest creating a fake email that makes it look like your email was bounced back to the sender. Something like:

> This is an automatically generated Delivery Status Notification.
>
> Unable to deliver message to the following recipients {your email address here}, because the message was forwarded more than the maximum allowed times. This could indicate a mail loop.

Change your settings so that this e-mail is sent out to every email, every time. Make sure you invite the IT guy out to get drinks so that he has your back.

Faux Work Keys
You know all those keys you have in the kitchen drawer? Spend 99 cents on a package of colorful key organizational toppers and create a ring of keys that looks official. Leave them on your desk. If they get stolen, no problem! Otherwise, people will assume you are at the office and locked in a utility closet on the second floor. Besides, everyone knows that people who have keys are important.

The Call In
Ensure that on your desk is a red file marked "Princeton Account." Fill it with some official bullshit paperwork. If you are running late, call in to your boss' secretary and have them "look up" some information in that folder for a meeting you are at. Make sure you whisper in the phone like you just stepped out of said meeting. Also make sure there is a twenty dollar bill in the very back of it in case you need to bribe the secretary into reading the same bullshit document for the fourth time.

Full Cup of Coffee
No one, not even the laziest person, will leave a full cup of coffee at their desk. Take the top off your Starbucks so that the fullness is apparent. For the very clever, make a fake whipped topping with some insulation foam and white paint. Stick it on top the coffee for added effect. With that sitting on your desk, everyone stopping by will assume you have just stepped away.

Invite!
Quit being a chump and sneaking around the office! Invite everyone out for a 3:00 p.m. drink at the local bar. Buy the first round. Be a hero. Then, fake a phone call from your sick aunt and get the hell away from your stuck up co-workers.

Comic
Where Thunder Comes From

List
Five Worst Types of Wingman/Wingwoman

Simply put, the wingman or wingwoman is there to ensure you get laid. They help find a suitable partner at a bar, they talk you up and then they know when to leave and/or take one for the team by banging the ugly friend.

Of course, then there are the wingmen that completely screw everything up.

The Married Wingman

No one is getting laid tonight.

If you have completed your wingman duties in the past, you may find that most your friends have found a partner, married and left you behind. Sadly, you must then make do with the married wingman, the saddest of all wingmen. Sad in part because they are looking to find you a good partner instead of a good lay. This causes them to pass over some of the better catches in favor of something a bit more attainable. You'll also find that the married wingman has marriage regret and will just get angry around potential lays, especially when instead of getting laid with the other girl he has to possibly sit up all night with her and "talk one for the team." As this is not desirable, he'll fake a call from the wife and head home early, leaving you to fend for yourself.

The Puker

This is the wingman that forgets to drink a lot less than you. Just when things get interesting, he pukes on your target's shoes. Either that or he does make it to the bathroom, but reeks of vomit and chases any potential birds off. Girls are nicer and will at least hold their wingwoman's hair while she reverse yawns in the stall. After puking, no wingperson can make a full recovery and it's best to call it a night.

The "Making sure everything is all right" Wingwoman

"Time to go."

There is nothing worse than a wing that does not know their duty. This one falls under the wingwoman category more than it does guys. While a girl is chatting it up, her wingwoman swoops in and drops a, "Just checking in and, hey, Blahblahblah is here and wanted to say hello," while pulling at her arm. Maybe later she interrupts and mentions that the two girls haven't had a chance to talk all night. There is nothing more annoying than a wingwoman not only neglecting her duties, but keeping a girl from potential hook ups.

The bait-and-switch Wingman

The classic wingman failure. It's the end of the night and the man has found a girl and the girl has a friend, but your wingman is there for you. The wingman is getting ready to take one for the team when he pulls the man off to the side and says, "Hey, I like girl A better. How's about a switch and you take girl B?" If you say no, the wingman gets pissed and bails, leaving you with a pissed off B and an A that needs to walk her home. If you say yes, the girls will pick up on this and diss you both. The Bait and Switch is a no-win situation.

The cock-blocking wingman
The night has gone great. The man has found *the* girl with the wingman's help, the wingman has talked the man up and he's prepared to take one for the team and be with Girl B. The night is ending and they all make plans to get one last drink before heading home. The man heads to the bathroom and on his way back, notices that he wingman is deep in conversation with Girl A. As he approaches, wingman holds his arm out and blocks the man from the last bit of the conversation. The Girl A's mouth is wide open in surprise and she backs away. In less than two minutes, both girls pack up and leave after revealing that wingman wanted to sneak out with the man's girl. In one fell swoop he has ruined everyone's evening. You try to explain but the chick just punches you in the face for hanging out with such an asshole.

Thanks, Wingman.

Collection
You Suck, Joe Show

It was September 15, 2001 and everyone was still reeling from 9/11. We were standing in line outside the Newport Music Hall in Columbus, Ohio to see David Byrne. It was his Look Into the Eyeball Tour. As we waited, a loud religious nut, perched on a milk crate across the street, was prophesying the end of the world. Many people in line wanted to make his prophesy come true. I think everyone just wanted to escape for a little while. Jesus dude was not helping.

We got inside as the opening band was finishing up. I bought a 32oz beer, which is a great buy because you don't have to get in line as often. Problem is that the beer gets piss warm, so you have to chug it. Then you have to go stand in line for beer. And for the bathroom. We made our way to the front of the room and found a spot, stage right, back about 20 feet.

David Byrne and his band sauntered out in gas station outfits, embroidered names and all. They played.

It was the best show I had ever seen. Still is.

It could have been the mental state that we were in or it quite possible was the best show ever. Either way, we were all floating a few inches above the sticky floor. I get goosebumps thinking about it.

Then at the midway point of the concert, the music stopped and Joe Show came out on the stage. Joe Show is a DJ at a local Classic Rock station that was sponsoring the show. For some reason, Joe Show was holding his bowling league's season wrap up party at the concert. He grabbed a mic and talked up David and the band. He then started in about his bowling league and how special it was to him.
The audience plunked back down on the sticky floor and began to mumble. He then asked David Byrne to help him hand out bowling trophies to the "winners" in the bowling league. He handed David a card with names on it. David seemed slightly amused and a bit nonplussed at the whole bit. Well, it was the Midwest. The crowd was pissed. Yells at Joe Show started. "Get off the stage!" "You suck Joe Show!" "No mo' Joe Show!" Add a smattering of boos and profanity and Joe got the idea. Joe took back the list from David and sped through the last bit of the trophy handing out. He cleared the stage, but not before handing out other bowling trophies to David, the band and the string section. You rock, Joe Show. Really.

Regaining composure, David jumped back into the show. In about thirty seconds we all forgot about Joe's self-indulgence. Again, the show rocked.

A few days later, I was reliving the story about the concert to my co-worker, Kindra. On a side note, I mentioned the whole bit about bowling and trophies. She suggested I write a letter to the editor of the local alternative paper. So I did. The letter to The Other Paper went like this:

An open letter to Mr. David Byrne:

Please accept these apologies from myself and the hundreds of others who attended your concert Sept. 15 at the Newport Music Hall. It seems that a local radio station thought it would be appropriate to distribute their bowling league trophies in the middle of your concert, bringing the momentum of a tremendous show to a screeching halt.
I can only congratulate you for recovering that momentum with grace and style, making the second half of your show even better than the first. Please do not hold the actions of a few against the rest of us. We definitely want to see you back in Columbus.

Doug

P.S. Idiots! Screw you Q-FM 96. And you suck, Joe Show.

I sent the letter in on a Monday. The weekly paper comes out on Thursday and my letter was not in the editorial section. I was disappointed, but not surprised. I had expected to get a phone call from the paper asking me if I actually existed and if they could print my letter. And I mean really, who cares about David Byrne anyways... Time passes.

The phone rang at 6:10 a.m. It was the next Thursday. The letter had been printed.

(Who knew?) The call was from the morning jocks on the radio station in question. They wanted to get me on the air with Joe Show and poke fun at him for his antics. I said it was too early and I had to get ready for work. "How about 9:00 a.m.?" Yeah, I can do 9:00 a.m.

Yeah! I was going to be on the radio and we were all going to make fun of Joe Show. Hurrah! I called all my friends to tell them to listen in to the verbal beating.

Little did I know.

Around 8:45 a.m. they called me. They quickly reviewed what they wanted to go down. Waggs and Elliot would introduce the bit, ask me for my side of the story and then bring Joe Show on to mock him. Easy. I waited on hold, listening to the DJs banter as DJs do. Then I was up. They spoke about the letter in the paper and read some excerpts. I was introduced and gave my side of the story. We all laughed. They then said that there was someone on the phone who wanted to talk to me.

"Doug, you are a dick." Joe Show has a way with words.

Joe told his side of the story. He claimed several things:

1. I was a dick. (I can see that.)

2. He, out his own pocket, paid for the 60 or so bowling leaguers at the concert. (I had accused him of using free passes that could have gone to real fans.)

3. He claimed that there was no booing and that everyone in the audience LOVED the trophy ceremony. (No comment.)

4. He said that the trophy handing out to David, the band and the strings was done by him running home before the concert and gathering up 10 of his personal trophies. (I can't dispute this, but who the f*ck would want a trophy with Joe Show's name on it?)

5. He claimed that David Byrne had come up with the idea about handing out the trophies. (Oddly enough, I can believe this. Byrne is an odd cat. My issue is that Show should have said thanks, but no thanks. Of course, egotistical assholes could never say no to an opportunity like that.)

And then the verbal beatings ensued. As Joe Show described his lame ass side of the story, I tried to interject with my interpretations of his recollections. The entire morning crew and Joe Show attacked and ripped me sideways. I didn't have a chance. They didn't want to poke fun of Joe Show, they wanted to make me look like an ass. Sadly, it worked. The volume on my phone was turned down and no one heard my witty comebacks. I ended up looking like someone who punched a quadriplegic in a wheel chair on her birthday.

At the end, I hung up and called my wife. She was very supportive. "Honey, they made you look like an ass."

Two years later during a reunion at Ohio University, my buddy Larry said he had heard me on the radio six hours earlier. I said that was impossible. He was positive. When his alarm clock radio went off in the morning, there I was, talking about the David Byrne concert and how Joe Show had screwed it up. Turns out it was a "Best of QFM-96." Yeah, the best of. Larry said, "They made you look like an ass."

Sigh. David Byrne has not been back to Columbus since.

YOU SUCK, JOE SHOW!

(Author's note: Joe Show unexpectedly died in 2016. As soon as I heard the news, I felt bad for the resentment I held for him all those years. Whenever I got to tell this story, I remember explaining what an asshole Joe Show was and in my mind, what an asshole he still was. After he died, there was an outpouring of positive remembrances of Joe and of all his work for charity and local music. This is my opportunity to tell everyone that I was not happy with Joe Show that night and for many years after, but that I forgive him. It was all for entertainment, both on his side and mine. And while this story is not a glowing memory of Joe Show, it is a memory and it is the only thing I can give him now.)

Comic
Jesus As A Child

Ask HolyJuan
How to Build a Mancave?

Dear Holy Juan,

In a few short months I will be getting married. This means my future wife and I will be moving into a new home soon. You've given advice on moving, keeping your wife happy, even parenting lessons (which I will undoubtedly need someday). One topic I have yet to see addressed? The home oasis of every American male. I'm talking about the Man-cave.

Holy Juan, I will need a Man-cave in my new home. Since I've never been married or a proud home-owner before I am at a loss. Does a finished basement automatically become the Man-cave, or will I have to flip a coin with my wife to see who gets dibs? If the basement is unfinished, but I use my considerable talent to change that, is it automatically mine? Will a shed in the backyard suffice as a Man-cave? Can I even hook up satellite TV to a shed?

My only solace in our current condo is the computer room/ office which I share with my fiancé and there's a goddamn poster sized picture of Marilyn Monroe on the wall. It's not even a sexy or seductive one either. This trend cannot carry over to the new house.

Help me, Holy Juan. You're my only hope.

Sincerely,
Mr. Phip

Dear Mr. Phip,

Buying a home can be a very stressful… wait… you are getting married? Married? Have you thought about the repercussions of this? You realize that when you are married, you lose the right to
say "man." Everything after that is "us." What you are asking me is how to build an "Us-Cave."

How To Build An Us-Cave

Step One: Buy a house
Make sure your house has a basement or second bedroom. This way you can fill those large, unused spaces with the boxes of sports memorabilia and man crap that you will not be allowed to unpack.

Step Two: Watch Home Improvement Shows
By watching home improvement shows, you will start to begin to gain confidence in your abilities to think about how great it would be to have an Us-Cave. Please note, you will have to record the Home Improvement shows and sneak out of bed in the middle of the night to watch them.

Step Three: Reminisce
Soon the DVR will be filled with other shows like "The Biggest Loser" and "The Real Housewives of Atlanta" and "16 and Pregnant" and there will be no more room for DIY shows. This will give you plenty of time to sneak into the spare bedroom and sort through the boxes with your old Xbox One, baseball cards and baseball gear. Weep quietly to yourself now. Do it in the baseball glove so that with every sob, you inhale the sweet, sweet smell of bachelorhood.

Step Four: Construction!
Surprise! Your wife sold all your man crap and now the spare bedroom is empty (actually she threw the shit out and the guy with the trash truck just made a cool $1,500 off your collectibles.) Time to think about filling this now empty room with stuff! You repaint. You re-carpet. You buy a bed and an end table and a set of drawers. What's this? A recliner! And your wife allows you to buy a 44" LCD, Wi-Fi enabled flatscreen. Your Us-Cave is almost a reality.

Step Five: Mother-in-law moves into the Us-Cave
And before the smell of wet paint is gone, your wife moves her mother into your Us-Cave. Now, all that is left is to await death. I'd suggest eating two pounds of bacon a day to quicken your inevitable end, but now that your wife is vegan, so are you. You'll live to be 100. Until then, mother-in-law needs her colostomy bag emptied. Get to work, Mr. Phip.

Congratulations on your pending nuptials!

How To
How to Hide Your Pregnancy

You are pregnant and you want to hold off telling the world for a few weeks. Most of your co-workers and friends have accused you of being pregnant before, but they were just guessing. Now they would be right, but it's none of their business. Here are a few tips on how to hide your pregnancy.

Pregnancy Test Tricks
Run out and buy a set of pregnancy tests. Keep one in your purse. Ensure that you accidentally pull it out whenever your curious co-workers are around. Act embarrassed and say a lot of "oops!" and quickly hide it away. Keep suggesting that you are tired of buying them every month.

Take the second test and have your husband pee on it. Unless he's pregnant, it should come up negative. Rinse it off and keep it in the cabinet. If you are going to have friends over, stage it in the trash can. Leave the empty box in the medicine cabinet for your curious friends to find.

The Purse
Everyone notices when a woman takes her purse into the bathroom. It means only one thing: she's on her period and not pregnant. Ensure that you take your purse to the bathroom on every trip. It's even better when you leave it at the table and then come back for it a few seconds later.

The Calendar
Use your home and work calendar to track phantom ovulation dates. Only track it a few weeks in advance and don't fill up the calendar. Fill in fake body temperatures for added reality. Drop a couple 99.3s in there for excitement.

Drinking
If you are a good mother, you'll have quit drinking as soon as you found out you were knocked up. Your friends are used to you knocking back a few Capt. N' Diets at the bar and are now curious as to why you are refraining from drinking. Try these methods and excuses:

Faux Cohol: ask the bartender for a coke in a tumbler with a lime. It looks like a mixed drink and you can pound 8–10 of them before you start to get woozy. You can also order cranberry and soda or have him put a NA beer into a pint glass.

Hold and dump: if someone buys you a drink, put it to your lips for show. Later, take it with you to the bathroom and dump it out. Go to the bar and buy a Mormon Mother and a drink for your friend. Don't get them mixed up!

Antibiotics: if someone catches you not drinking, tell them you are on antibiotics and cannot drink for seven days. At the end of seven days if you get called out, explain that you missed a few doses and you have to go back and retake the whole series again.

Fertility Drugs: If for any reason you get called out and find yourself stumbling… lay out that you are very embarrassed; but that you are taking fertility drugs and that you cannot drink while on them. The key to this is using you initial hesitancy as fake embarrassment. Tell the person to keep it a secret so that you can ensure they will tell everyone.

Smoking
Yes, you need to quit smoking if you are pregnant. If anyone asks, just say that you are planning to be pregnant soon and you'd rather quit now than later.

Emotional
You might be a bit stressed out with the whole "living creature in my belly" thing and it might come out in tears or possibly rage. This is an easy fix; just tell people that you have been trying to get pregnant for the past X months and you are getting fed up with all the tips and tricks that everyone keeps telling you. They'll get the hint.

Puking
This is easy: say you had White Castles (Krystal) for lunch. No one will ever disbelieve you, especially if you use this excuse four days running.

How To
How to Make It Look Like You Are Cool for Cheap

Sometimes, being cool is way too expensive. Here are some cheap and easy ways to make it look like you think you know what might actually kinda hip (with associated costs in parenthesis.)

1. In the signature of your e-mails, add a "01+" to the beginning of your phone number to look international. (Cost: free)

2. Post fake "Missed Connections" about yourself on Craigslist after a night out with your friends. Post anonymously on the internet and e-mail it around to your co-workers. (Cost: free)

3. Rename all the contacts in your cell phone address book with the names of famous celebrities like Paris Hilton, Fergie, Jay-Z and Rick Springfield. Leave phone out on table in front of friends. Every time phone rings, apologize and say you have to take this call. Note: Delete Heath Ledger. (Cost: free.)

4. Buy a replacement handle for a guitar case. Use the screws to attach some broken wood to the replacement handle. Stagger around the subway with fake blood on your head and tell people you fought off some biker dudes with your guitar case. (Cost: $4.50 for the handle and $1.25 for the Halloween fake blood. $.75 for a guitar pick for added reality.)

5. Mail yourself notes composed of cut-out letters from magazines glued to a piece of paper, with no return address. Tell your friends you have a stalker who can't let you go after sleeping with you just one night. (Cost: $29.70 for a year's subscription to Bridal Monthly.)

6. Carry the "Zen and the Art of Motorcycle Maintenance" around with you and let it fall out of your bag at opportune moments. (Cost: Go softcover and you'll pay $0.01 + $3.99 shipping on Amazon. Do not go uber-cheap and buy a version without the cover from the ½ priced bookstore.)

7. Answering your phone in fake French (Cost: free if you watch enough Monty Python on PBS.)

8. Conduct fake insider-trading cell phone conversations with your "broker" advising him that he's f'ing crazy to try and dump your Commodore stock. (Cost: free, unless you really did own stock in 1994.)

9. Use multi-colored markers to make several marks on back of hands. Smudge liberally. When people ask, explain you were clubbing until 5:00 a.m. in (large city two time zones away.) If they ask for details, say Hef gave you some roofies and you can't remember much. (Cost: stop by a group of people preparing protest signs and ask to borrow markers.)

10. Keep Euros in your wallet (Cost: With current exchange rates, use three, five euro bills: $21.75)

Comic
If Jesus was a Woman

- It's a miracle!
- Is there anything these Crocs can't do?
- This is an abomination to God's Temple!
- I know, but did you see the sales? You can't get doves for that cheap anywhere
- John and James, you sit over by Simon. Judas, I want you where I can see you.
- You call this pain? You try having a baby Mister.. that's pain!

HolyJuan.com

List
Free*

I am officially done with advertisements that say "Free," but that are not. This basically means every free advertisement. Free is a very specific word. It means something that costs nothing. Free should not have any words following it to explain what you have to do or pay to make the product/service cost nothing. I am going to send letters to my representatives to try and get the following "free" items taken care of.

Free! (plus shipping and handling and processing and service charge)
This type of free is big on television. You buy one item and you get a second free. Free as long as you pay for shipping and processing, which I assume are jacked up high enough to actually pay for the second item tenfold.

Free attachments! (plus shipping and handling and processing and more service charges)
This is very similar to the first Free except that during the commercial, they show you the original item and then they demonstrate how it works using several attachments. Those attachments are Free… as long as you pay S&H&P&Handjobery)

Free 30-day supply! (With purchase of 90-day supply)
There have been several commercials on television and radio that suggest you can get a free 30-day supply of diet or sexual enhancement drugs. That's great, except that you have to buy a 90 day supply to get the 30 day supply free. And pay shipping. I assume the ingredients in the pills of both varieties are the exactly the same. If a manufacturer wants to send you some free pills then they should be free with no strings attached. Not that I need sexual enhancement drugs. And I would need way more than a 30 day supply of diet pills.

Free*
Screw you asterisk. No matter what you say or how you politely suggest… you mean that free isn't. I hate you, asterisk.

Buy one, get one free!
I do the shopping in the HolyJuan household. We have a collection of about 30 meals that we rotate through. On the nights that Miss Sally wants to have linguini with Alfredo, I make myself chicken wings as Alfredo make me nauseous. So I watch with a keen eye as the prices of 64oz of frozen chicken wings goes up and down. They usually float between $6.99 and $7.99 for 64 ounces. Then every so often, my local store jacks up the price to $12.50 and does a BUY ONE GET ONE

FREE. That's crap! If the gasoline companies fluctuated their prices like this, the pitchfork and torch people would be rolling in stacks of money. With this mentality, everything is buy one-get-one-free if you pay 2x for the first item.

Free shipping and handling
Bullshit. All that cost is rolled into the final price.

Free checking
OK… it might be free, but don't overdraw your account or you'll be paying for everyone else's free checking. Oh, and it really isn't free because your money is being used by the bank for other purposes. Everyone looks the other way so that you can continue to get free checking. You can get an interest-bearing checking account, but the people that can afford to put that much money in their checking account can afford to pay for checking anyways.

Free (but we sign you up for a membership that sends you overpriced shit you don't want or need)
I watched a "Girls Gone Wild" commercially very intently, rewinding and rewatching to ensure I had all the details correct. As it turns out, you actually have to pay for the videos. So I zipped up and turned the channel until I got to the "Free Software" commercial. In this one, they suggest that you can get a video of your choice for free… but you have to give your credit card number and agree to buy a new video every month. If you are getting something for free and giving up a credit card number, you deserve what you get.

Free hand jobs
This one is completely false and I ended up having to pay $15. And the dude couldn't make change for a $20.

Collection/How To (Not really a How To, but it's in the title)
How To Sleep in Chicago

I love Chicago. My buddies Doob, Doug, Dave and Paul all live or have lived there. Great food. Great people. Lots to drink and all hours of the night to drink it in.

I had the fortune of heading up there for a work related training in the Summer of 2005. My boss and I drove up from Columbus. The hotel was in one of the 23,546 suburbs of Chicago that ends in the word Park. We were meeting the client at a Cubs' game and had to take a very complicated way of getting there. We threw our bags on the hotel room floor and drove a number of miles over to my boss' friend's house. At the house, we picked up three other guys and took someone else's car to a train station. We rode the train for about 40 minutes and got off at a very non-descript station. We walked about 8 blocks to a bar and had a quick three drinks. (Drink count: 3) We tumbled out of the bar and crammed into a cab (Note: we = 6. Luckily, I was the only fat f*cker.)

The cabbie was kind enough to take a few short cuts and the locals accused him of trying to find the worst traffic to raise the meter. I don't think Apeluriphediakni spoke much English. We made it downtown via curbs and sidewalks to the Cubs' game.

Ah, the Game! The Cubs were playing the Red Sox for the first time since 1918. I'm not a huge fan of baseball, but this was a big game and everyone in town teemed with excitement. Our company paid for all the guys plus the client to go to the game. (Client = smoking hot MILF in her very early 40s.) Todd, one of my boss' friends, explained that we would be "standing on the curb" at the game.

Standing on the curb turns out to be exactly that. There is a concrete curb that spans the bleacher seating area. A chain link fence follows down the middle of the curb around the upper walkway and dead ends into the stands. There is standing room only along the walkway, so to gain an additional 6" above everyone else's head, you can stand on the curb. The problem is that there is only about 3" of curb to stand on, so it is necessary to hold on with one hand to keep your balance. This proves tricky when attempting to drink your fifth draft beer (Drink count: 8) and eat a brat with mostly everything on, beside and under it.

Game ends. Cubs lose. (Drink count: 9ish)

We immediately head over to a bar called Sluggers. Sluggers is an all-in-one alcoholic stop. It's got batting cages, dance floors, pool tables, duelling pianos and Capt. Morgan's. And Jell-O shots. And Bacardi. And various liquors that when mixed together taste like either a candy apple or Dr. Pepper. (Drink count: unknownish) We got hammered as my boss flirted with the client.

At some point later in the evening, I decided that I wanted Taco Bell. Ta-da, there was a Taco Bell next door. I did not tell anyone that I was going to go to Taco Bell because that would involve me actually speaking. At the Taco Bell, I used a number of mumbles and various hand signals to order about 14 burritos. I took them back over to Sluggers and sat outside the entrance on the step and ate. And ate.

Minutes passed and no one I knew came out of the bar. I stumbled back into the bar and looked around for about ten minutes. No one I knew was there. I was alone in Chicago.

I called my boss on his cell phone. We both slurred at each other for a minute or two. The rough translation of the conversation is as follows:

ME: "You leave me alone at bar."
BOSS: "You not in bar. We go."
ME: "You bang client lady?"
BOSS: "Me bang client lady soon."

That son of a bitch. In an effort to get back to the hotel to f*ck the client, he left a soldier behind. F*cker. He said that the hotel was a Marriot in something something Park. I repeated, OK, Marriot something something Park.

I stopped at an ATM and got $200 out. At least I have a timestamp on a receipt. 2:47 a.m. I stopped a cab and asked him to take me to the Marriot in something something Park. He had no idea where the heck I was talking about. I attempted to explain that it was in a suburb. I let someone else get in the cap and called my boss to get better directions. He wouldn't answer. He did not answer for the rest of the night. Banging the client does that to you.

In my drunken state, I assumed I could walk to my friend Doob's apartment. I mean, how big could Chicago be? As I stumbled through the neighborhoods and surrounding shops, I called my boss several times to explain how I was discontented and that I wanted to no longer continue our work relationship. (I said that he was a f*cker and that I was quitting and flying home the next day and that he was F*CKED.) I tried calling Doob, but he didn't answer.

After about another hour of walking, I gave up. I wasn't going to find Doob's and my boss wasn't going to answer his phone. I needed to sleep, so this is what I did:

I found a house that was under construction.
There was an alley next to the house.
In the alley there was a pile of gravel, a stack of 2x4s and some demolition materials.
I stole a newspaper off a neighbor's porch.
I spread out a layer of newspaper in the center of these construction materials. A nest.
I lay down.
I covered myself in the rest of the newspaper.
I slept.

I woke up at about 6:00am. I had no idea where I was except that it was outside. That was f*cked up.

Sat up and it all (well, some of it) came oozing back. The game. The bar. The taco bell. The walk. The quitting. The nest.

I got up and started walking. Again. This time, I listened for the 'L' and found a set of elevated tracks and followed them to a station. I bought a ticket (how the hell did I get $200 cash?) and rode the train west to the last station. I got off and re-boarded on the eastbound to downtown Chicago. Once I made it downtown, it was about 7:00am and I called into the office back in Ohio. I got the address of the hotel from Lori who didn't ask any questions. I had to write the address down using a cigarette butt and the ATM receipt. I stopped a cab and he drove me $75 to the hotel in Orland Park.

When I got there my boss was not in the room. He was still with the client, taking one for the team. (He took another one for the team the next night, too. F*cker.) I slept again.

I did not quit. I did not fly home. Later that evening, at the training, my boss mentioned how funny my messages about quitting were. I laughed, knowing I had meant every word.

Ask HolyJuan
Dear HolyJuan: Can I remain friends with a Trump voter?

Dear HolyJuan,
I just found out that my friend is going to vote for Donald Trump. I really like this person and I would like to remain friends with them, but, I mean… they are going to vote for Donald Trump. Any advice?

Signed,
Concerned Friend

Dear Concerned,
If there's one thing I have, it's advice. Except now.

There is no real good answer to this question because it really wasn't a question. Your only question was, "Any advice?" and I didn't really even answer that question.

Let me turn your email into a question for you:

Dear HolyJuan,

Should I remain friends with my friend who is going to vote for Donald Trump?

Signed, Better Question Asking Concerned Friend

Dear Better Question Asking Concerned Friend,
The short answer is no. No, you cannot remain friends. Unfriend them from Facebook, Twitter and Instagram. Delete their email address. Rip up any photos. Avoid the same strip clubs you used to frequent together. Burn the digeridoo they gave you for your birthday. Format the area of your brain in which their memories are saved. Finally, delete the nudes from your phone that they accidentally sent you one drunken night and you never told them. One last look, then delete.

The longer answer is yes, of course you can still be friends. You can't let silly things like political leanings ruin a friendship. Friends get through tough times. Friends have each other's back, even when you start to doubt their sanity. You will still be friends… but you will be turd- eating friends. What I mean by that is imagine that you caught your friend eating a turd… you accidently walk on them in the bathroom and they are knees down in front of the toilet with a turd half in their hand and half in their mouth, munching away. They turn and look at you, brown faced. You say you are sorry and back out. You never mention the turd eating again. You both pretend like it never happened... but it did. You saw it. And every time you look at that friend, you will think about the turd eating. About what kind of frame of mind they had to be in to eat a turd. About how many turds they've eaten since. And if they eat turds, what else will they eat? You will still be friends... but you are friends with a Trump voter. I mean, a turd eater.

Yes, you can remain friends with someone when they say they are going to vote for Trump. I just wouldn't kiss them.

Love, HolyJuan

Comic
Jackson Pollock Venn Diagram

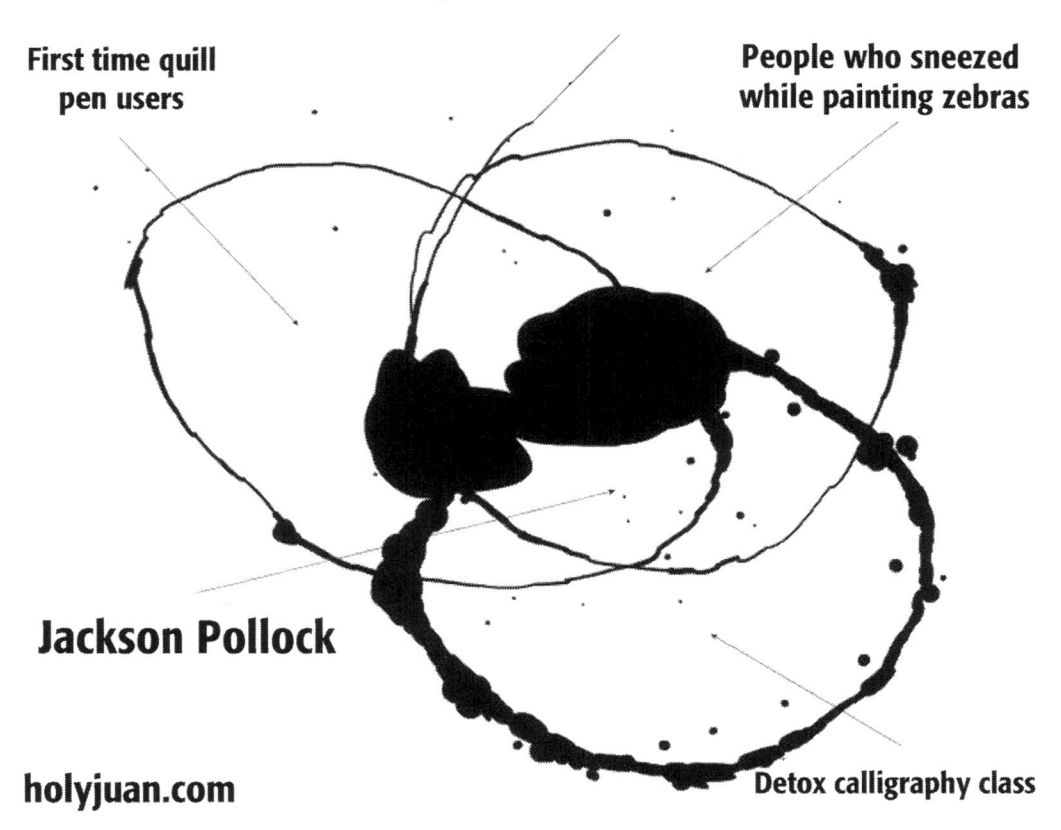

First time quill pen users

People who sneezed while painting zebras

Jackson Pollock

Detox calligraphy class

holyjuan.com

List
Phrases a Man Does Not Want to Hear from a Woman

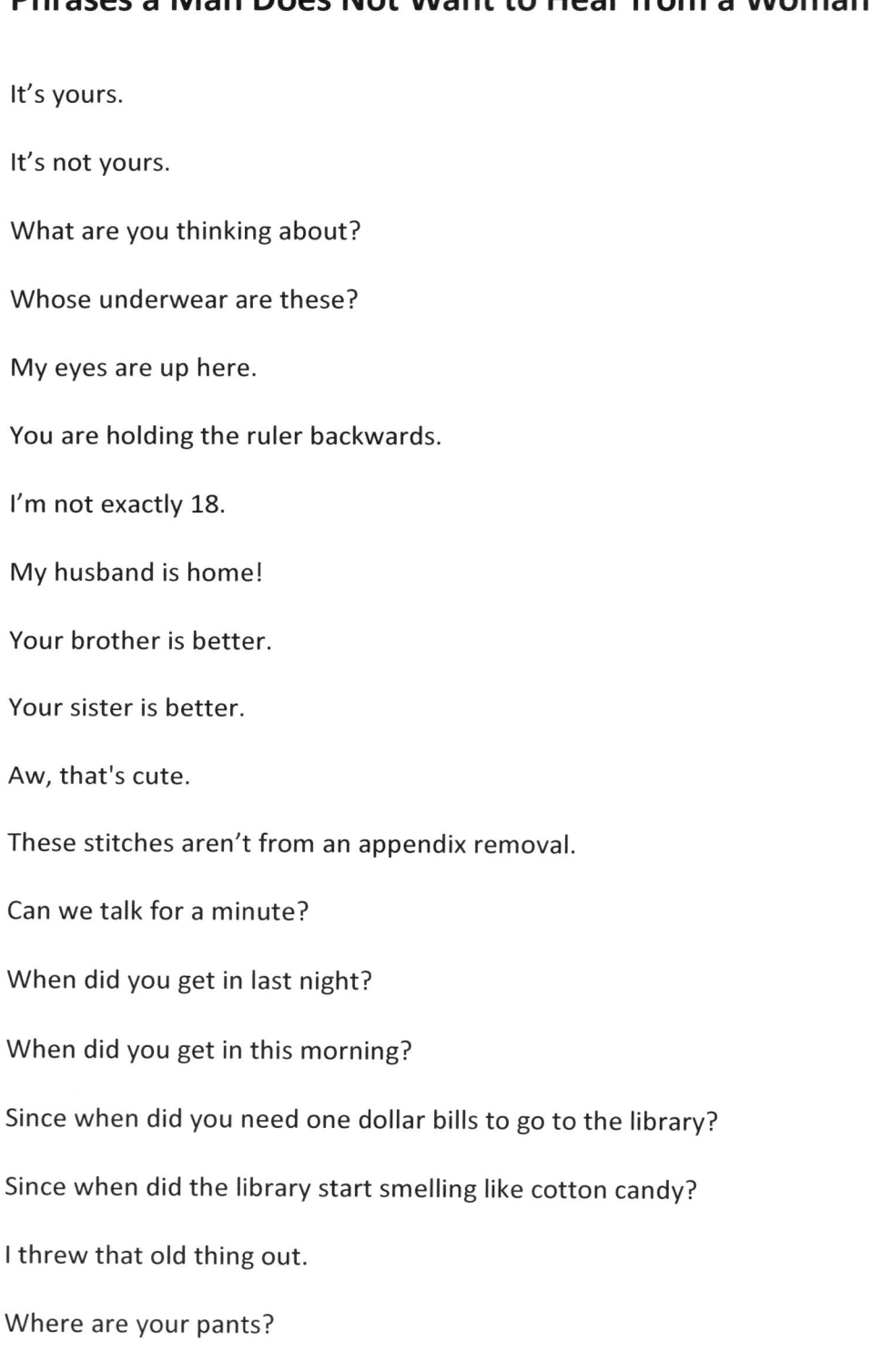

It's yours.

It's not yours.

What are you thinking about?

Whose underwear are these?

My eyes are up here.

You are holding the ruler backwards.

I'm not exactly 18.

My husband is home!

Your brother is better.

Your sister is better.

Aw, that's cute.

These stitches aren't from an appendix removal.

Can we talk for a minute?

When did you get in last night?

When did you get in this morning?

Since when did you need one dollar bills to go to the library?

Since when did the library start smelling like cotton candy?

I threw that old thing out.

Where are your pants?

Does this make me look _____ ?

You left the seat up.

I also have something I need to tell you about my past.

Can I come out with you and the guys?

Is that porn?

Can I have the other credit card?

My brother needs a place to stay for a while.

What lab results are these?

Why do you have condoms when I am on the pill?

Where are you?

Collection
The Fight that Never Was

I will tell this from my point of view. There were a few other points of view, but I am not one to assume or fill in the blanks for others, especially since I was a little drunk at the time.

Here's the publicly released version of the story:

Handsome Joe awoke the morning after Jeff's bachelor party. He got out of bed, left the bedroom, but soon returned to get his glasses. He tripped over a rocking chair and split his face open. Fast forward six stitches. That is that.

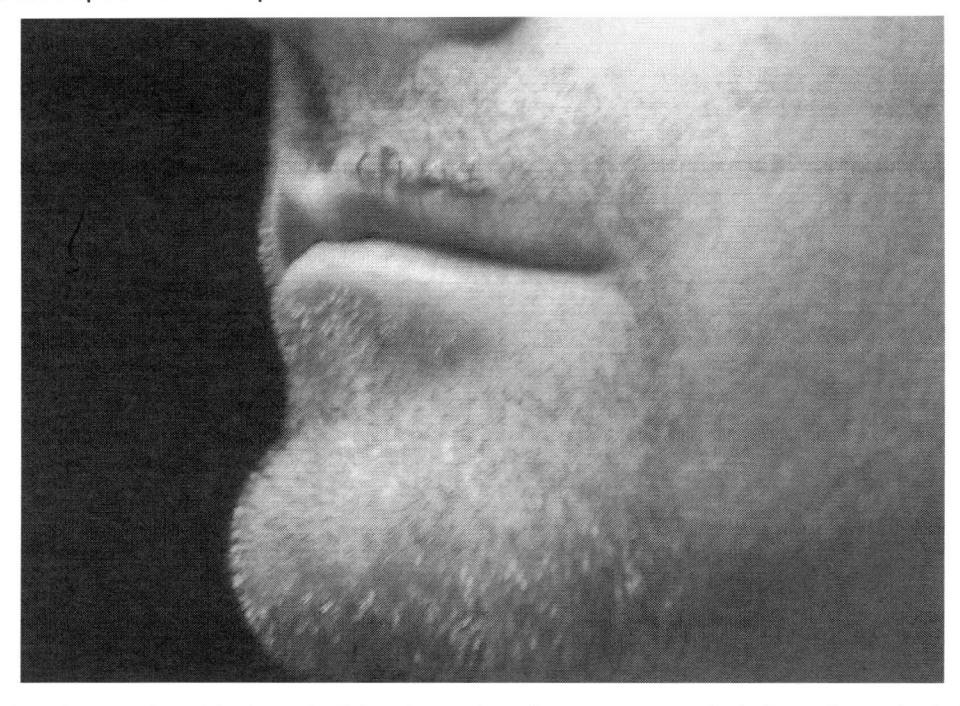

It's hard to see in a black and white photo, but there are several stitches above Joe's lip.

I have a different version of the story. Slightly different.

It was Saturday night and Jeff's bachelor party was still in full swing. We had stopped doing what we will not mention and left the place we will not call attention to, to meet up with his fiancée and brother's wife at a club.

The club is a nice little dance place that plays very typical dance music. When you are drunk and dancing with your friend's brother's wife, it is a lot of fun. After an hour or so of dancing, Jeff and company finally decided to call it a night and left. I was on my own. Made my way over to the bar and ordered a drink so that I would have something to do while I watched the 23 year old girls dance. (Yeah, I'm that creepy guy.) I finished my drink and decide not to order another. Walked up the stairs and to the exit. At the top of the stairs is a vestibule that leads to a side bar or through double doors out to the street.

And there was Handsome Joe. Right outside the upstairs bar. I thought Joe had left with the others. Joe was involved in a conversation with some dude. The dude was unhappy. The dude had a frowny face and a uni-brow. The two universal facial expressions for a fight. Joe claims the guy was six foot tall. I won't take that away from him.

Joe was trying to calm the guy down. But at the same time it seems that he was trying to egg the guy on. I remember Handsome Joe saying in his soothing voice, "Hey. Calm down dumbass." Joe had his hands up in front of him in either the "I give up" or "I'm going to shove your ass backwards" position. It was escalating.

Here's the "I think I remember" part. Joe put his hand on the guy's chest. The guy threw up his own hands and pushed Joe back. Joe regained his footing and stepped forward.

I sucker punched the guy.

I am not one to fight. I am not one to sucker punch. The sucker punch is a very cowardly act. The dude had no way of knowing that I was there. He had no way of seeing me throw the punch. Makes me an ass. But hey, don't start shit
with Handsome Joe when Doug's had a few drinks and is sexually frustrated.

My fist connected. That was the second thing that happened. The first thing that happened was that I totally missed the side of the dude's head and glanced off his cheek. Then I connected, with Joe's face.

A split second later, I was grabbed and shoved out the door by a very large man. I turned to see where Joe was, but the very large man yelling at me persuaded me to walk away. I waited down the street. Any drunkenness I had was gone in the rush of adrenaline. Joe appeared and turned up the street in the opposite direction. I ran across the street to avoid the club entrance, ran up and back across and caught up with Joe. He had a napkin pressed up against his face. The napkin was a little white and a lot red.

Handsome Joe laughed. "Doug. You punched the wrong guy."

The next day, Joe's wife made him go to the Urgent Care. Fast forward six stitches. That is that.

Now, I must tell you that both versions of this story are out there. To save Jeff embarrassment that a pseudo fight broke out at his bachelor party, we tell, with all honesty, that Handsome Joe lost a fight with a rocking chair. That is the truth.

List
Ten Reasons Why I am a Better Parent Than You

1. Our kids do not have and will never have access to television in their rooms.

2. Our kids do not have and will never have access to video games in their rooms at bedtime.

3. Our kids are only allowed to drink beers from local breweries and not corporate, factory beers.

4. We eat dinner as a family.

5. Our children were taught at an early age how to clean their needles and how to rotate their hidden injection sites to prevent collapsed veins.

6. We require the kids help with house work and yard work for an hour a day.

7. The kids memorize the way out the back of restaurants or out restroom windows for a successful dine and dash.

8. The children are trained to know which cars are expensive and thus more profitable with which to fake an accident on their bike.

9. The kids switch nightly helping with the preparation of dinner.

10. Manners are required at all times. "May I be excused," and "Please hand over the wallet."

Collection
My Glasses

Years ago I went to an eye appointment by myself without any spousal support. I am nearsighted (slightly blind) and wear contacts. I also wear glasses when I'm not wearing the contacts. Because I do not wear my glasses out in public, I really do not care what the frames look like. So when the sales lady at the glasses store pointed me towards the $200 frames which were next to the $350 frames, I pointed at the small rack of forgotten, dusty frames in the corner.

"How much are those frames?"

"Those? Um, they vary. The prices are marked on a sticker on the arm."

I found a pair for $40. "I'll take them." She was not impressed.

My wife was also not impressed when I brought them home a few weeks later. But I didn't care. I only would wear them in the mornings for a few minutes or on lazy Saturdays.

So for many years my glasses had gathered dust, worn only five or six times a year. I was actually hoping that if I waited long enough, the frames might come back in fashion.

But then we put a television in our bedroom and everything changed. I'd put the sleep timer on the television and fall asleep to thirty minutes of Comedy Central. To do so, I must wear my glasses. Most the time, I remove them at the last minute before falling asleep. Other times I wake up in the middle of the night with them still on and I remove them. And sometimes I find them in the bed or on the floor the next morning.

One morning I found them in the bed. I also found them on the floor. Like a mother panda, I rolled over on my glasses in the middle of the night and they broke at the bridge. I tried to glue them, but there wasn't enough material and there was too much torque for them to hold. I tried watching TV at night with one side held down to the side of my head by gravity and the other held up, wedged between my head and the pillow. That worked as long as I didn't move which didn't work at all.

Miss Sally suggested on several occasions that I should get new frames and that she would go with me this time to help me decide (i.e. pick them out for me.) I said I would, but never have… because I fixed my glasses!

Using a brightly colored pencil with smiley faces on it and tape, I MacGyver-ize them back into perfect working order. Here is a photo of them:

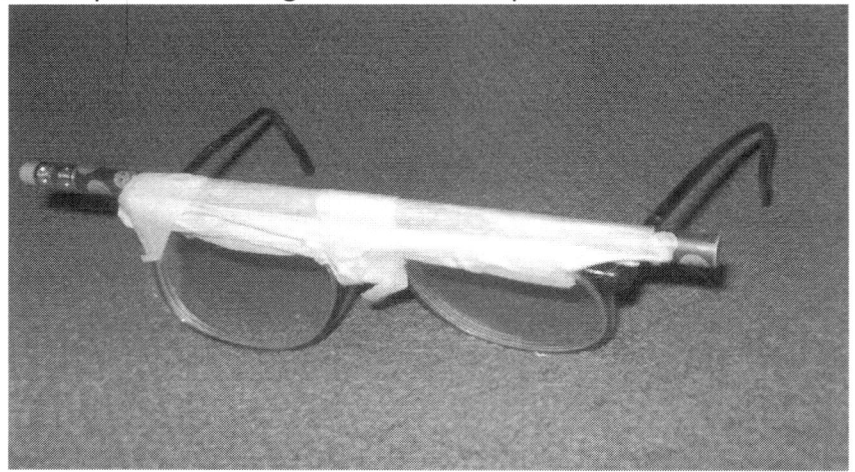

Just like new!!

I have only made it downstairs with these on a few times when I didn't want to put my contacts in. And they have only been outside once on a lazy Saturday when I went to get the mail. My neighbor was mowing his lawn and either did not see me or thought I was shot by a tape arrow.

I am surprised that Miss Sally has not thrown them in the trash. I think Miss Sally realizes that the only way go get me to buy new frames is to watch me embarrass myself to the general public. So here it goes.

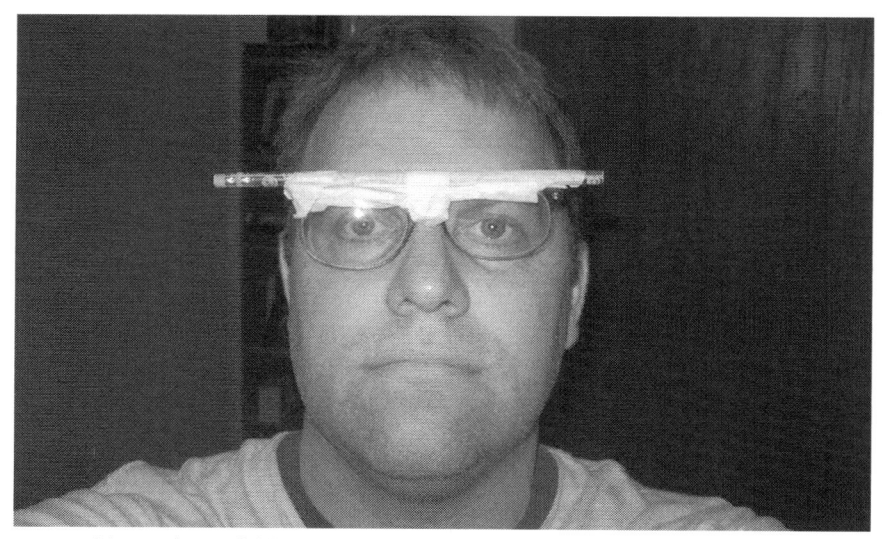

New glasses? Who needs new glasses! These work just fine.

I'm thinking about sharpening the pencil so that at night, I can write down and remember my very special dreams.

List
REAL College Essentials

Screw the laptop and mini-fridge. Here are the real essentials that every college student should own.

Shampoo bottle pee detector
This device is embedded in your shampoo and/or conditioner cap and beeps to let you know when someone has peed in your shampoo bottle. It happens more than you think and your shiny hair isn't always because of rinsing and repeating.

Condom wrapper gum
These innocent pieces of gum come in packaging that look like condom wrappers. If you are not getting any, you can leave them laying around and act like you are. If you parents are visiting and find real condom wrappers, you can say they are gum. If you are banging a chick and smell wintergreen, you might want to pull out before you "blow your bubble."

Marijuana/daisy hybrid plants
This plant looks like daisies, but smokes like marijuana. Grow weed without getting caught. Give your boyfriend/girlfriend a gift that keeps on giving. Comes with Baby's Breath rolling papers.

Stall saver
A necessity for the dorms. Fake boots and pant legs that sit in the bathroom stall so you can save a spot for yourself for the cafeteria food induced ass explosion. Those other schmucks will see the boots under the stall and wait for the "person" to finish as they listen to the pre-recorded grunts and groans that emanate from the hidden audio player. After lunch, just walk by those suckers waiting in line and pass the time with the rolled up playboy in the boot.

"Walk-of-shame" survival kit
This kit includes: change of clothes, sunglasses, aspirin, map of campus, list of pillow talk conversation starters and fake phone number. (See Sorority Girl Initiation Kit for pregnancy tests.)

Practice sheep genitalia

Great for hopeful fraternity rushees. Don't look foolish when confronted with a sheep for the first time during rush week. Use these ultra-realistic sheep parts to work on your grip and trust technique.

Cum stain sheets
These sheets make dorm sleeping tranquil. 300 thread count, Egyptian sheets are pre-printed with cum stains to ward off agile roommates looking to hook up in every nook and cranny of the dorm room.

Sorority girl initiation kit
Comes with "Freshman 15" weight scale that automatically deducts fifteen pounds, 'Idiot's Guide to Faking That You Like IPAs,' and twelve pack pregnancy tests.

Collection
The Lumberjack

Handsome Joe invented a drink called The Lumberjack. He didn't invent the word lumberjack or the drink or the glass that it comes in, but he combined all three and that's all that counts.

I met a few friends at a bar that was at least two notches higher than my calling, but I went anyway. When I got there, everyone was drinking out of glasses with tall, thin stems. The kind of glass that forces you to stick your pinky in the air.

Handsome Joe had no glass in front of him. I asked why he wasn't drinking. He said he was and the waitress would soon be returning with his drink. He said I should have what he was having… The Lumberjack. The Lumberjack? That sounds pretty damn manly for that bar. Would this drink be on fire? Or perhaps have a whole cactus in it? Maybe it came served in a hollowed out log with a pine cone floating in it.

The waitress returned and said, "Here's your Lumberjack." It was a frosted beer mug filled with a pink liquid. I asked the waitress what was in it. She said vodka (manly,) cranberry (not really manly) and Triple Sec (downright girly.) I asked her what drink it actual was. She said, "It's really a cosmopolitan." Joe said, "It might be a cosmopolitan. But if you can convince the waitress to give it to you in a frosted beer mug, then it is The Lumberjack, is a lot manlier."

How To
How I Make Comics

I love to make comics. While images say more than words, words and images together do doubly so. (Except for those motivational posters. Sigh.) My problem is that I cannot draw consistently. There are only a few shapes that I can replicate. That's why many of my comics have stick people in them and why Jesus looks different in every comic I make. If I have an idea for a comic, I try to make it in a single panel. But sometimes, I have to create several panels to get my idea across. My solution is to use a scanner and Photoshop.

Here is a scan of how I built one of my favorite comics, "The Baconizer."

On the left is the idea written out with handwritten content. On the right is what I drew to be photoshopped. The drawing on the right has every element that the comic needs. Once I scanned this one image, I pasted it four times and then erased the bits I didn't need then added text.

In the end, it looked like this:

> **Panel 1:** "I came over as quick as possible! Show me the BACONIZER!!" / "The bacon goes in here..."
>
> **Panel 2:** "..and GOLD comes out on the other side!"
>
> **Panel 3:** "Oh. I thought it worked the other way around."
>
> **Panel 4:** (silent)
>
> holyjuan.com

Sometimes I draw the faces and put all the mouths to the side with some additional eye expressions. But as you look at all my panel comics, you will either see very random sketches of the same person or exact cut and paste images with ever so slight differences.

Doug may not be an artist, but Doug is a clever boy.

List
Life Should Be More Like T-Ball

In T-Ball, everyone gets to bat once an inning.

In T-Ball, the last kid up automatically gets a home run.

In T-Ball, you can play in the dirt and not get yelled at.

In T-Ball, it's pretty good if you can throw the ball and even better if it is in the general direction of where it is supposed to go.

In T-Ball, getting hit by the ball doesn't hurt that much.

In T-Ball, there is no score.

In T-Ball, fans clap for pretty much anything that happens on the field, no matter which team does it.

At the end of T-Ball, there is a snack and a drink.

And at the end of the T-Ball game, there are two game balls to give away and even five year olds can do the math that tells them that someday, they'll get the game ball.

Getting the game ball is pretty cool.

Collection
Panties Just Don't Do It For Me Anymore

I used to love the word panties as much as I loved panties themselves. Panties. It's a fun word that elicits excitement and opportunity or at least it used to. The only reason to talk about panties was when a girl was getting into them or, hopefully, out of them. And imagining if the panties matched the bra or maybe even no panties. No panties!

Panties!

But now... panties have lost their luster. When we were potty training our daughter we used the word "panties" all the time, "Ann pooped in her panties!" or her yelling in defiance, "NO PANTIES!" No panties used to be good. Now it means a two minute chase around the house and five minutes more of wrestling them on. I never thought I'd have to fight a girl to get her panties on.

I've rinsed out poopy panties in the sink. I've watched my daughter gleefully point out Dora the Explorer on her panties. I go to pick them up off the floor and realize she took them off because they were wet.

Panties. Not fun anymore. Goodbye panties. Next up: having to dislike bras.

List
The REAL 13 Things Your Pizza Guy Won't Tell You

I read an article on the **13 Things Your Pizza Guy Won't Tell You**. They were pretty much bullshit. Here's a list of the REAL 13 things the pizza guy won't tell you:

1. The sauce really stings the open sore on his finger.

2. The cheese that misses the pizza and lands all over the place will make it back on top a pizza at some point in the night.

3. Pizza ain't all he's delivering.

4. The soap is still out in the employee bathroom.

5. If you do not tip him well, your next delivered three topping pizza will have four toppings.

6. He does wish you would come to the door topless.

7. The delivery guy is not en route and you are going to get the next thing that pops out of the oven.

8. It is hard to wipe a runny nose with the plastic gloves on, but he'll keep trying!

9. 30 minutes or less is a suggestion and not a goal

10. Long, scraggly hair is in. Hair nets are out.

11. Its hard to catch the flying disc of dough, but luckily the floor has enough flour on it to keep most of it from sticking.

12. Pizza guy is always very happy and he always seems to have red, bloodshot eyes.

13. You won't believe some of the shit that will fit in the dough presser machine.

Comic
Get Over Her

Panel 1: "Dude, it's been three weeks. Get over her."
Panel 2: "Imagine your internet connection being down for three weeks."

holyjuan.com

Collection
What is Up with Bread Pudding?

Life is a lot like bread pudding: there are thousands of mediocre bread pudding recipes out there and only a few gloriously delicious ones, but you have to go through the bad ones to get to the good.

In 2011, co-workers Keegan, Allen and I were in Ft. Lauderdale for work. We decided to go down the street from the hotel for dinner at a very manly Irish Pub called Maguires Hill 16 – Irish Pub & Eatery. I had eaten there a few nights before with just Keegan and they had great food and beer. And for the second time, we had the surly waitress from Russia. At least I thought she was from Russia with her accent. I didn't ask and she was just surly enough to stab a fork in your eye for asking.

Allen asked her where she was from. And she said, "Alabama" and then it all started to make sense. After I told her I thought she was from Russia, she grew enamoured with us and we had a fun evening bantering with her.

At the end of the meal, she asked us about dessert. She offered up bread pudding, proudly adding that she made the dessert by hand and that there was really no question that we were going to order it. At the time, I had never had bread pudding because the stuff just sounds awful. It's the dessert invented to use up scraps of food that didn't get used in other meals; it's the chili of desserts. But she told us that we could get it with ice cream and I knew what that was.

So she disappeared in back and returned about 10 minutes later with a giant, glass sundae dish filled with dark bread infused with sugar and cinnamon, custard, ice cream and a whisky drizzle. It was glorious! The face you see in the original photo is of sheer delight. Of the conscious delay in devouring to just hold that moment of joy.

My first bread pudding was the best bread pudding I have ever eaten. It was thick without being dense. It was sweet, but not cloying. The ice cream and custard would normally clash, but the bread seemed to break up the fight and it was as if an Irishman, a Scot and a Brit were all having a merry time together knocking back shots of whisky drizzle. So delicious. So memorable.

And so the images you see of that face and bread pudding is me remembering that moment of exaltation and the hope that the next bread pudding will maybe, just maybe, be better than that first one. I think we all know there will never be a better bread pudding than that first one, but I will keep looking.

When you have the opportunity and feel daring, order the bread pudding and make the face. You can create your own variation, but mine is the wide-eyed, staring at the dessert, with flat hands held up to the lips to contain the excitement. For best results, get your face as close to the bread pudding as possible.

Maguires Hill 16 Irish Pub & Eatery is now closed and I will never be able to see that surly waitress from a small town in Russia called Alabama. And the best bread pudding in the world now has to be somewhere else and it is my job to find it. One gleeful photo at a time.

List
Things That Are Gone That I Miss

The older I get, the more things change and disappear. Some are my fault. Surprisingly, most aren't. Here's a list of the things I am missing from my life.

Marathon bars
Marathon was this great candy bar. It was braided caramel with chocolate covering it. It was very chewy. The commercials for it were of a cowboy having a chew out with another candy bar cowboy. `The longest lasting candy bar was declared the winner. Marathon cowboy always won.

Communication that you can control
When I was a kid, we had two telephones. One upstairs and one in the basement. The basement phone was the one I used to talk to girlfriends. Now our house has no phone, but my kid has access to internet chat, Facetime, in game chat and someday he'll have a headset to talk to strangers. When we had one line, my parents had a good excuse to kick me off the phone because if the house caught fire they would need an open line. Now, I need to make stupid excuses as to why he needs to get off the device. Usually the excuse is, "Because I said so."

Stick shift
I love stick shift. It gives you something to do while driving and keeps you focused on the road. With automatic, I've become a drone. We are a two-car family and my wife is not interested in driving stick, so both our cars are automatic. I don't blame her. Just need to get a job where I make enough to buy a third car.

Swedish Fish
I'm on a diet. Swedish fish are not part of that diet. I miss you Swedish fish.

John
John and I are best friends. But we both got married and I've got kids and he's got work (*now a few years after writing this... he's got twin boys!) and somewhere in the middle, we stopped hanging out. We talk every few weeks, both of us committing that well try to get together, both of us failing. I did call him, out of the blue, with a situation that didn't need immediate attention, but he gave it attention. We'll get our acts back together.

Four-hour hangovers
I used to be able to go out until 2am, sleep until 8am and be fine by noon. Now, I go home at midnight, get up at 8am and am miserable for 48 hours. If I go out on a Thursday night to Ladies' 80s, I am starting to feel like myself again on my Monday drive into work.

Not drinking
At some point in my life, I didn't drink. From 0–19, I assume I did other things that kept be busy. Now it seems that I can't go an evening without a glass of wine. I'd quit, but then I'd miss drinking instead of missing not drinking. I'll take the latter.

HolyJuan
I don't write enough anymore. I blame Fake Dispatch.

Being ahead of the technological curve
I knew Windows XP front and back. Now I can't figure out how to defrag a drive or figure out the problems my operating system is politely explaining to me. I can't stand tablets. I need a nice keyboard to be able to write. I assume my phone can make bacon, but I'll never know. I'm already looking out in the yard to see if there are any kids to yell at.

Zima
Screw you. It was crisp and delicious and a nice, portable alternative to beer. The photo below is from my sister. When she heard Zima was going out of production, she bought her local store out. She called me the day she drank the last one and we both cried.

Rumor has it that they might begin to make Zima again. I hope that you and I can crack two open together and use this book as a coaster.

Collection
I Had A Vasectomy Today

I had a vasectomy today. Here are the basics of how my day went:

Woke up screaming.

While getting the kids ready for school, I read the "Pre-Surgery" instructions. I learned that I was supposed to be scrubbing my loins for the past five days. I'm sure my cursory "soap across the balls" does not meet their definition of scrubbing.

Kissed Miss Sally goodbye and confirmed that she would be picking me up at noon thirty.

Got in the shower and gave myself a good 2 ½ days' worth of scrubbing action. By 1867 standards, I would be blind now.

I shaved my balls.

I got out of the... hold on, what? You SHAVED YOUR BALLS?

That's right. The instructions said to shave them and they got shaved. I pulled out my grooming kit. Knocked the shrubbery down as short as the guard on the electric trimmer would let me and then I jumped in the shower. Balls are not a good medium to be dragging a sharp blade across. And the reason I know this is because I spent a full 30 minutes bent over and staring at my ugly, wrinkly, bigger-than- average, dropped melon shaped nutsack. Men, don't ever examine your balls with your eyes. Check for cancer, but do so with your eyes closed. Women, kudos to you for even getting within three feet of that withered fruit, change purse.

Shaving balls is like trying to wrap a coat hanger around a whipped cream covered balloon. As soon as pressure is applied, skin around the man grapes distorts and deflects away from the blade. I found it best to stretch the loose skin in a tennis racquet stringer to create the proper tension on the surface. Let's just say I pulled things taut and did the best I could. Thirty minutes later, I was done.

I got out of the shower, got dressed and went to Target to buy tighty-whities like the instructions suggested. I also bought two bags of frozen peas and Swedish Fish. Back at home, I put on tighty-whities for the first time in 25 years. At least now tighty-whities come in different colors.

Sally picked me up and we drove to the doctor's office.

Checked in and only waited two minutes before being called back.

The doctor's assistant was very, very cute. We went to room #7.

She told me to remove my clothes below the waist and hang them up. It was then that I realized that she would be seeing my shaved balls and cold, shriveled penis. Usually, I bone up very easily and would be concerned/embarrassed about that, but I was nervous and cold and more concerned that the cute chick would have trouble deciding which was balls and which was penis.

I got undressed and sat on the table. She came back in and gave me a sheet to cover my shame. I laid back and she got everything in the room ready for the surgery. From this point on, I did not look down and instead counted the holes in the ceiling tiles.

Doc came in and we had some chit chat about the music on the radio and that he was going to feel me up like he did at the previous examination.

He then gave me a good scrubbing with some soapy something. I haven't had that kind of action from a guy in months.

Surgical pads were placed around my loins so that only my balls were showing. The pads had adhesive on them, but I didn't find that out until the end.

There was a shot, some numbing, a little pressure, a little more pressure some chit chat. Then another shot, more pressure, a lot of talk about my work and then it was done. Stitch, stitch. That quick. About fifteen minutes from the first numbing shot to doc walking out of the room.

Cute girl cleaned up and took the surgical pads off and hoo-boy they have a little stick to them. One of them had been placed right across the penis and though it didn't hurt, it was like a leash giving me a tug. And not the kind of tug you get at the Asian Spa at the airport.

Cute assistant left so I could get dressed. (I don't get this… she just was in close proximity to my junk for 30 minutes and she leaves so I can put my clothes on?)

She came back in and read me the TO DO and NOT TO DO, told me that swelling was normal, slapped me on the ass and shoved me out the door.

When I got home, I began rotating frozen peas on and off my groin every 20 minutes. I took Advil, though we picked up a prescription pain reliever just in case.

I played Wii. I watched Caddy Shack. I messed around on the computer. The kids came home from pre-school and Greg was as interested as a six year old could be about testicles and what the hell happened to me. He used at least five pronunciations for testicles and he slipped a "balls" in there once or twice with me correcting him to use the proper word.

I'm not sure where he learned to say balls.

Collections
RollerCoaster Tycoon Life Lessons

I pulled out our dusty copy of RollerCoaster Tycoon a few years ago and my son Greg and I play on and off. It's a computer game where users build an amusement park and run simulations of people riding rides, eating hot dogs and throwing up. Greg had just turned seven had really been getting into it. I sometimes need to help him figure out how to reach goals and maximize profits so that he can complete a level. We both love it when you do complete a level because any of the park guests with a balloon all turn to you, let go of their balloons and cheer.

One day, he was playing at the kitchen table and asked for help. One method to determine how well you are playing is to look at a list of all the rides and booths in the park and sort them by profit. By knowing what isn't profitable, you can change prices accordingly or tear down a ride to build another.

At the bottom of Greg's long list of rides and booths was a very lengthy segment of Balloon Stands that were all losing money. There must have been twenty Balloon Stands.

I said, "What are you doing with all those Balloon Stands? It isn't profitable! How much are you charging?"

And Greg replied, "I'm giving them away for free."

"You are not going to make any money doing that."

Greg said, "I know, but when I do win everyone will have a balloon to let go of and the sky will be filled with them."

Comic
Camel Through the Eye of a Needle

List
Ten Actual Han Solo Quotes That Sound Dirty

10. Thanks for coming after me. I owe you one.

9. No, no, no! This one goes there, that one goes there.

8. She may not look like much, but she's got it where it counts, kid.

7. Oh. I thought they smelled bad... on the outside!

6. Great, kid. Don't get cocky.

5. Besides, I know a few maneuvers.

4. Get in there, you big furry oaf! I don't care what you smell!

3. Great shot, kid, that was one in a million!

2. Now let's blow this thing and go home.

1. Sorry about the mess!

Collection
The Friend Tiers

My friend, Terry (Tier Two Friend,) and I were talking about friendship. How do you categorize friends? Aren't friends just friends? I say no. I think that friends are divided up into tiers. There's Tier One friends and then everything else drips down from there. Allow me to explain:

Tier One Friends: These are your closest friends. In fact, they are your most hated of friends. These are the friends that you have to deal with. If they screw up, you are there to hold back their hair while they puke or lie to the cops. You carry their baggage. You live their lies. You are there when they need you and there when they do not want you there. You forgive them. You forgive them again. You help them into rehab. You help them back into rehab. You loan them money and never expect to get it back. They make mistakes and you yell at them for messing up again. You dis all your other- tiered friends because they need you. You love them and you hate them. But best of all, they are there for you when you are throwing up or getting arrested or coming down off a black tar heroin binge. You cannot get rid of them and they cannot get rid of you.

Tier Two Friends: These are the best friends. You can hang with them. You can listen to their woes without getting involved. You help them when they need a hand, but if you've got some other pressing issue, they understand. They are there for you when you have a flat, but you would never expect them to do more than call AAA. They loan you money and expect you will pay them back. They know when to walk away. They know when to leave you alone. Tier Two friends sometimes make it to be Tier One friends, but you hope they don't. These are the people that help you move when you buy a new house, but don't ask to live in the basement.

Tier Three Friends: These are your Tier Two friends' friends. You see them at the grocery and you only talk about the common friend. They are the work friends that will someday be Tier Two friends, but not today. They wave and say hello, but don't ask you about anything more than the local baseball team or work-related issues. They will bring you back lunch if it isn't an inconvenience. Sometimes they think of themselves at Tier Two friends and you listen to them patiently and then promptly shove them into the Tier Four Friend category.

Tier Four Friend: These are the people you have to be friends with. Your neighbor who keeps harping on your mowing technique. The parent of your kid's friend who does not share the same basic set of interpersonal communication skills. All religious leaders. Most real estate agents. At night you secretly dream of killing them.

Tier Five Friend: Anyone on Facebook who does not fall into any of the above category. They are idiots and you have no clue why you even still interact with them except that they were born in the same year as you and you graduated at the same time.

List
10 Ways to Pretend that you are Straight

I do not believe there is any way to "un-gay" yourself, so you better get used to it. But there are several ways to mask your gay so that your friends and family will think you are straight. I have several friends who are closeted gays and I have helped them to sequester themselves way in the back behind the luggage and the backup ironing board. So with the assumption that you are a gay dude, here are ten ways to hide your man gay:

1. Become a religious leader
No one would ever suspect that a religious leader would be gay. This identity will allow you to hide your sexuality AND persecute others who are brave enough to live their lives. Be careful about over persecution... We all know what confessional those guys are kneeling at.

2. Wear Wranglers
Gay guys would not be caught dead in Wranglers. Even the guys in Brokeback Mountain wore vintage Lee jeans. Wranglers are straight man camouflage.

3. Build "Ships in a Bottle"

This isn't gay, it's just odd. Concerned family members might attempt to get you dates or involved in social clubs, but they will never suspect your sexuality.

4. Drive a bland, American car
Nothing screams gay like a man driving a 2012, yellow VW bug. Hide yourself behind the wheel of a 2002 Ford Focus. No air freshener or fuzzy dice. A dashboard compass will enhance the illusion. Make sure there are fast food wrappers on the floor and the maps should be folded incorrectly.

5. Don't eat sushi, calamari or plantains
Those foods sound gay to the uninformed. Also, be careful at Asian restaurants. One order of Moo Goo Gai Pan and your work buddies might start asking questions. General Tso's Chicken is a sure bet, straight man's food. Just make sure you mispronounce the Tso part. Better yet, go to Chick-fil-A.

6. Keep your cash folded lengthwise
By keeping your cash folded lengthwise, everyone will assume that you have been or are going to the nudie bar. When you do pay with cash, tuck the bill into the cashier's waistband. If it's a guy cashier, smell the bill as you hand it over and say, "Smells like cotton candy my friend. That's the one that almost got away."

7. Hang out at the hardware store
CAREFUL! As many gay men read my website, you may all pack up, head out the door en mass and end up clustering in the plumbing isle. Spread out. Don't look at the cabinetry or the appliances. Stick with hand tools or hinges. When a friendly customer service person asks if you need help, reply loudly, "What? You think I'm gay or something?"

8. Don't have an opinion
At parties, especially during an election year, political and social debate may arise and you might be confronted with a question about same sex marriage or gay parent adoption rights. It's best to curl your lip, act kind of squeamish and say, "I don't really have an opinion." You may think that gay-bashing is in order at this time, but I think we all know that those who bash the loudest are over compensating.

9. Talk about how great a president Ronald Regan was
Simple. Easy. 100% effective. Again, you need to walk a careful line on this one. Don't talk about Nancy's clothes or how rugged Ron was in his earlier years. Drop "Cold War" a few times and how disappointed Regan was that he never got to nuke the shit out of anyone. Just shake your head and mumble, "Good ole days."

10. Have sex with women
I know it's gross... but sometimes desperate times call for drastic measures.

Collection
Hole Story

It began innocently enough. I was crashing an after-work drinks event of a company I didn't work for anymore. Bobby was there and, as an ex-worker, he was also crashing the party. After a few hours of drinking, the party was on the move to another bar and the sensible people were heading home, while the not-so-sensible people were deciding on the next venue. Bobby was getting ready to head home while I was keeping an ear to the conversation about the next bar. He asked me, "Did Ralph tell you about the hole in his hotel room wall?"

(Author's note: You will see "Ralph" in place of this person's name. As this is recent and involves work, I need to keep his name secret. If you know who Ralph is, keep it to yourself, but feel free to bring it up to him.)

"Ralph did not mention a hole in a hotel room, go on."

A few weeks previous, Ralph had been on an installation. The install team was staying in a very nice hotel due to its proximity to the site and room availability. We usually stay in nice hotels during our installations, but I think this was the very nice kind of place that didn't just put a mint on the pillow, but would unwrap it, fold it into the shape of a bunny and then put it in the guest's mouth and help them chew.

After a long day of work, Ralph was in his room watching a mix martial arts fighter on his device. The fighter was performing some kind of kick that take years of practice to master and Ralph thought he could pull off that kick. Ralph practices mixed martial arts and could easily kick my ass, so practicing such a move wasn't strange for him, even though he was slightly drunk. So he attempted the kick and succeeded in putting a foot sized hole in his hotel room wall.

Oh, shit.

This was a big deal. Investigating the hole, Ralph thought to himself," I could make up some story about how the hole was made, but no one would believe me because I am Ralph. I could tell the truth, but I am Ralph and I just can't see myself getting this taken out of my paycheck. So, because I am Ralph, I will fix it myself. "

And so this is what he did: over the next few days, he hid the hole with a chair and kept his Do Not Disturb sign up, keeping the folding mint guy out of the room. He secretly snuck out between the end of the work day and dinner to purchase spackle and spackle applying tools and fixed the drywall. He applied layers of spackle at night and sanded them in the morning. With a loose chunk of the wall available, he took it to the hardware store and had matching paint made. This was applied on top primer and blended in to match the existing texture. After four days, the hole did not exist. This was such a coup. From a possible $400 damage-charge to an almost perfect looking wall.

And Ralph would have gotten away with it, except that he told Bobby. Trusted Bobby. And I tell you the following as a truth and not as some fake addition to this story... I rubbed my hands together in delight at the thought of trapping Ralph in a prank. Ralph is a clever guy who is just suspicious enough to avoid getting caught up in my pranks. But I had a foolproof plan.

The next morning, I sent out an email at work. I wrote it in such a way that it sounded like it was going out to several people, but I only blind copied Ralph on it.

It went something like this:
"Hey, I am blind copying you all on this because I don't want to get anyone in trouble. Admin just sent me an invoice from a hotel chain for damage to a room. It only says the chain and not the hotel, so I can't specifically determine which project this would go to. All of you stayed at this hotel chain in the past few months, so please let me know if you know what this is. I wouldn't blink an eye, but the bill is for $1580."

And then I waited for Ralph to start sweatingI don't know why, but I got a lump in my throat and had to turn away.
was no immediate email in return, so I waited an hour before trying to run into Ralph. He was down in the shop and I got him and another worker to look at an issue we were having with a structure. While the three of us were looking at the issue and wrapping up the conversation, I said to Ralph, "Did you happen to see the email I sent?" With an absolutely, innocent straight face he said no and walked away. Damn. It was very likely that he had been in the shop and not checked his email in the past hour. I would have to wait a little longer.

But then Ralph waved at me from a distance and beckoned me over. His face transitioned from everyday mirth to a wide eyed gloom. "I saw the email. I think that was my room. Is the damage really $1580?"

"Yes. What happened? "

"I accidentally put a hole in the wall and tried to fix it, but they must have discovered my patch."

"Wow. Listen. I'll try to cover it up, but it's $1580! I'll let you know how it goes." And I walked away. Smiling.

A true prankster would have waited a day before telling Ralph. But I could only hold out 15 minutes. I tracked Ralph down. I walked up to him and shook my head. And then I said, "Hey, I ran into Bobby last night. Guess what story he told me about."

Ralph flipped between anxiety, knowing and relief in about two seconds.

Fortunately, his relief drop-kicked his rage and I did not immediately find myself in an arm bar or with a bloody nose. The great part about Ralph is that once he realized it was a prank and he knew he wasn't in trouble, he wasn't pissed. Since that incident, he's shared the story with several people at work and had not sought revenge… yet.

If any of you ever need a drywall guy and home security, I know a guy.

Comic
Wheel of Fortune Interview

So, you'd like to apply for Vanna's job on the Wheel of Fortune? Let's see your resume.

Ding!

Impressive!

holyjuan.com

The Last Story In The Book
The End of HolyJuan?

HolyJuan is dying. He's like the pasty white version of E.T. Still alive, but only just so. I blame Fake Dispatch, but there is more to it.

When I started writing in 2006, I had a backlog of stories that I wanted to tell. They just seemed to fall out of my brain, through my fingers and on to the page. I've tried to record my stories on tape or use voice to text, but there is something magical that happens when I type. The words in my head travel down my arms and when my fingers start to hit the keys, there is usually something new or clever that makes its way on to the page. These stories that were just memories always seemed to get better once I translated them from hazy recollections into these words.

I thought that at some point, I would run out of stories and then I would close up shop. But HolyJuan started to write new stories based on everyday occurrences using the same trick of telling stories with clever language and unusual observations. I could use my words to make many of the things I found interesting, also interesting to my readers.

Then advertising dollars came along. I was able to post ads on my page and every one of my faithful readers tickled tenths of a penny into my pockets. While I loved my readers, I needed to expand my audience if I was going to make any money. I started to write articles that would be interesting to those millions of other people out there on the internet through reddit, Fark and Digg. And as it turns out, those people aren't usually interest in Doug stories. They want lists, lies and comics. Easily digestible content. For this kind of writing, I would need to come up with a clever idea. And once I had that one little clever bit, I'd have to flesh it out with more clever ideas. Soon I'd have a solid article or list or rant or fake story and I would publish it and link to it on the major news aggregate sites. This would take several minutes or several hours depending on what kind of article it was and how much Photoshopping I needed to do to Sarah Palin/Barack Obama/Hungry Man TV Dinner box. I would then sit back and track all those incoming IP addresses, waiting for the cash to come rolling in. In my best year, I think I made $150. But then it stopped being about the money. I was addicted to the views, to the number of people coming to the site: the gratification from knowing people were reading my words.

Then Twitter came along. Instead of taking a nugget of an idea and developing it into an article, I can just post that one idea. The feedback was instantaneous. My ego was quickly rewarded and I didn't need to go through all that work of posting to HolyJuan. Soon, all my quick clever ideas were going to Fake Dispatch and HolyJuan was only for actual stories or comics. In 2008, I peaked with 374 postings on HolyJuan. That's more than one per day. In 2010, I still had a healthy 219 postings. But in 2011 when Fake Dispatch came to life, that dropped down to 72. By 2016, I had 10 postings. Meanwhile, over on Twitter, Fake Dispatch posts five to ten times per day. Quick bits of funny that don't require HolyJuan to succeed.

HolyJuan is not dead. But he's no longer the proficient rascal that he once was. My true fans/readers are mad that I stopped writing and posting as HolyJuan. Many of them don't like Twitter and so they have scattered to the winds with no HolyJuan content to read. There are a number people now know HolyJuan only as the character on Facebook that repeats everything that Fake Dispatch says.

But I need HolyJuan. I need him because sometimes I need to test something out or I get the itch to write something with more meat on it than 140 characters. I also need it because I use HolyJuan all the time to search for memories. I can tell people, "Search for 'holyjuan' and 'porn button'," and they can find the story I'm talking about. Plus, there are a ton of great stories on HolyJuan that did not make it into this book. Those stories are still out there along with the great comments. But I think that my next step will be to keep writing with HolyJuan on one shoulder and Fake Dispatch on the other. This time with publishing in mind.

HolyJuan is not dead. And he's not pasty E.T. He's more like force ghost Obi-Wan Kenobi—there when I need him and there when I don't think I need him. And when Fake Dispatch crosses over, he'll join him like Darth Vader did. But not the young Anakin Skywalker, he'll be the old grizzled, white James Earl Jones Vader version. Because we all know that HolyJuan and Fake Dispatch might be enemies at times, in the end, they are nothing without each other. And I need someone to blame for all of this.

Made in the USA
Middletown, DE
17 April 2017